The Bluebonnet Child

The Bluebonnet Child

Finding Grace in Poor Soil

Meggie Lee Calvin

RESOURCE *Publications* · Eugene, Oregon

To: Annika

Thank you for loving on Henley + other kids so well. You are making a huge difference!

♡ meg Calvin

Resource Publications
An Imprint of Wipf and Stock Publishers
199 W. 8th Ave., Suite 3
Eugene, OR 97401

www.wipfandstock.com

PAPERBACK ISBN: 978-1-5326-1959-5
HARDCOVER ISBN: 978-1-4982-4597-5
EBOOK ISBN: 978-1-4982-4596-8

Manufactured in the U.S.A.   JULY 7, 2017

Contents

Permissions | *vii*

Acknowledgments | *ix*

Introduction | *xi*

Chapter 1   Defined | 1

Chapter 2   Rooted | 4

Chapter 3   Biblical Bluebonnets | 8

Chapter 4   The Bible Tells Me So | 11

Chapter 5   Supplemental Hope | 15

Chapter 6   The Triple A Approach | 20

Chapter 7   Be Aware | 23

Chapter 8   Advocate | 35

Chapter 9   Articulate | 55

Chapter 10   Stories of Promise | 68

Chapter 11   Apocalyptic Assurance | 73

Chapter 12   Follow the Call, Make a Call | 78

Chapter 13   A Guide for Discussion | 82

Bibliography | *89*

Permissions

Acknowledgments

First of all, I would like to thank God for daily guiding me in my vocational calling of leading children from troubled homes into the healing arms of Christ. The words of these pages are Holy Spirit-inspired. I am merely a messenger. This book is my attempt to boldly declare the Good News. I found hope on each page, and I pray you and those in your care do as well.

My heart overflows with gratitude for my husband, Garrett. After hearing the sermon form of, "The Bluebonnet Child", you encouraged me to do more with this theme. You emphasized the need for its message to be heard. You are my life-vest that keeps me afloat in the waters of ministry. You are the epitome of comfort and fun to me. You nurture my identity outside of my role as a Children's Pastor, and then cheer me on as I get back to it. While my divine calling will sustain me in my career, you deserve a piece of the credit as well; because as my boss once said, "You have to get a life *outside* of the church if you want to survive life *within* the church. Now Go Home!"

Speaking of my boss, I wish to thank my Senior Pastor, Dave Smith. His example daily sets an *extremely* high standard for all of us who are called to serve in the local church. I aspire to write and lead as well as he does someday. He, along with Beth Wilke, Brenda Hargrove, Chandra Snively, and Lindsay Wilke also served as editors along the way.

I wish to thank my grandparents and parents for strengthening my roots despite the varying types of soil through our growth as a family.

The staff, Children's and Family Ministry Teammates, and parents of the First United Methodist church of Winfield deserve a standing ovation for their dedication to offering God their absolute best. I am nothing without my community of faith, and they have all helped in molding me to be more Christ-like. They are mighty partners in ministry.

Words can never express how thankful I am for Matt Wimer, Brian Palmer and all of the amazing staff at *Wipf & Stock Publishing Co*. Their professional wisdom, patience and encouragement have been true blessings. I also want to thank my copy-editor, Amy Graeser, for joining me (a complete rookie) on this literary adventure. Thank you to Lisa Buffum and Steve Wilke for not only offering a self-publishing course at www.beadisciple.com that originally launched this book, but for also letting me teach "Bluebonnet Child" courses on your formative website. Want to dive deeper into this book with an online community? Join me at www.beadisciple.com!

Lastly, I would like to thank my daughter, Henley June. You have poured so much love into my heart, that it has naturally overflowed into the lives of the children I serve. You are mine and your father's greatest gift and I will daily strive to live up to my most honorable title—'parent'. My prayer for you is that you will revere how God wired you and *boldly* follow your vocational calling (whatever that may be). May your conviction of God's love be such that it also overflows into the lives of others. Aim to cultivate the life-giving light of Christ EVEN in darkness, remembering that darkness *cannot* overpower light (John 1:15).

Meg

Introduction

FOR YEARS I HAVE followed the Holy Spirit's call on my heart to serve Bluebonnet Children. This call has led me to Bethel Seminary, community partnerships with like-minded organizations, and nearly a decade of serving as a Director of Children and Family Ministry at a mainline church in the heartland. Families of all types and talented children's ministry (kidmin) volunteers have spoken into this calling. With each lesson planned, Fall Teammate Training accomplished, or new faith milestone reached, the Bluebonnet Child has remained at the center of my heart. How will this new initiative affect them? Will the message it portrays overshadow the message they receive (or will not receive) at home? We are taught that the parents are the child's primary faith nurturers, and it is our role as children's pastors to partner with them; but what happens when a child's parental unit is neglectful or abusive?

Building up the local church to serve as a supplemental family to the Bluebonnet Child is not only my calling-it is also the church's. While we cannot completely alter the home-life of a Bluebonnet Child, we are called to serve. The Children and Family Ministry Team of any church can serve as catalysts, who lead the entire church in answering the call. My hope is that Children's Pastors and their teammates will see this book as a tool on the path to their holy dreams. (And as you read, please join the conversation on social media by tagging your posts with #bluebonnetchild.)

I composed this book with you in mind—yes, you. You who have a heart for meeting each child's unique needs. You who roots for the underdog. You who finds it offensive when others say, "Those kids are *too* loud/*too* energetic/*too* silly." You who loves learning about how children best learn. You who light up when the coolest fifth grader knows all the dance moves to a praise song and is not afraid to show it. You who tear up some mornings while praying for your students because the love you hold for them is too much for one little prayer journal to contain. And you whose days are beyond full, but you still aim to make them fruitful so you bought this book. This. Book. Is. For. You. It is intentionally short, because I can only imagine how busy you are. It is bursting at the seams with high quality resources, because I know you have high standards. And it contains questions to help you or a small group explore the distinct needs of your ministry, because while we are all in this together, only you and God know what is best for your church. May this book inspire and inform you as you move forward with faith and intentionality.

Chapter 1

Defined

SOME OF MY MOST beautiful and beloved memories as a child are of gardens. My grandfather and father are fantastic gardeners, and our family get-togethers were always adorned with lovely landscapes. Gardening is a craft requiring patience and intentionality. One must be careful of the depth and the width when digging. The quality of the soil is also key. The amount of water and sunlight varies from plant to plant. Some, like hydrangeas, require transplant during different seasons. Other plants, like orchids, need wire wrapped around them for support.

Then there are plants like the Lupinus Texensis, or as all of us know it—the bluebonnet. What a beauty! Growing to 6–18 inches tall, they sprout velvety light green leaves and gorgeous bluebonnets. I loved driving to school when I was a kid, for these covered the fields by Texas highways.

Bluebonnets grow like wildflowers. There is something unique about the bluebonnet. Unlike the first two flowers, Bluebonnets grow in the poorest, and most unkempt soil. One would never guess this from the bright, proud bonnets, but it's true. This flower's poor soil has never deterred it from producing lovely blossoms. Fascinating!

I believe that a small portion of people are like the Bluebonnet. Having no control over the soil in which they are planted, some people grow up in soils that are poor and unkempt.

I think of children from neglectful or abusive families as Bluebonnet Children.

You see these Bluebonnet Children most Sundays. They are running when they should be walking. How did they get to our church? Parents are nowhere to be found. The aroma from their pew is potent because of a lack of baths. They sneak extra donuts because they have not eaten much since the community meal on Friday night. They offer to help you clean up after Sunday school, because scrubbing glue off of the table with you is more enjoyable than what awaits them at home.

Kevin was one such kid. He was a Bluebonnet Child who was very aggressive. Whenever he arrived at our church pre-school program, it was only a matter of seconds before he would bite or hit. After a number of failed attempts to connect with his parents, I realized his father was not in the picture. Furthermore, his mother was having different men stay the night throughout the week. The energy of his home was not positive or stable. We were receiving Kevin into our programs at his most tired and delicate state.

After we knew his story, we adjusted our dance with him. When he first arrived, we started offering him a calm time of rest. This 20–30 minutes made a world of difference! Once he awoke he was more patient and happy. In time Kevin was able to articulate his feelings in a healthy way. Years have passed now and Kevin has grown into a very jovial and loving young man who attends our after-school programs.

Empowering the local church to serve as a supplemental family to Bluebonnet Children *is* my calling. Eternity-altering moments can occur at any age. I have met eight-year-old disciples who are more spiritually mature than their 47-year-old Sunday school teacher. Just as there is no set age for faith to blossom, life-scarring moments can happen at any age as well.

Think of how many adults struggle with a dark time in their childhood. Think of the sad hours spent trying to undo that moment—to rewrite that memory. Think of the emotional triggers that will not let one forgive. Think of how much time adults waste erasing the false images of faith that were painted for us as children.

Think of how this affects our relationships with others—our relationship with God. A big portion of my work is preventative in nature. I strive to nurture the young disciples of today on their path to becoming the spiritually healthy adults of tomorrow. A divine nudge guides me to assure that the truth of grace resounds louder than the dysfunctional tunes at home.

CHAPTER 2

Rooted

EVERY NIGHT MY DAUGHTER and I have a mini-worship service in her room. I doubt she would ever define it as that, but it is one in my mind. After we read books, and sing a lullaby or two, we rock a little longer just so I can get a good hold on the moment before it passes. A very artistic friend of mine painted an explosion of leaves on the ceiling above the rocker. It is *truly* the loveliest nook to read and rock. I used to pray while she was nursing (which in itself is a very holy experience), but now I carry her to her bed, tuck her in and then pray. With each stroke of the hair or scratch of the back, I say aloud the words of Saint Teresa of Avila.

> *"Let nothing disturb thee, nothing affright thee. All things are passing, God never changes. Patient endurance attains all things. Those who seek God shall never go wanting, God alone suffices."*

My grandmother shared this prayer with me and it is sacred to speak it with Henley. I then pray the Spirit would fill her with peace for the night and strength for the morning. And then when I sense my hovering over the crib has become borderline stalkerish, I quietly slip out. Like many other couples, our child was once a mere dream—a mere prayer that was somewhat unlikely. I am a carrier of trisomy 13, or should I say: I have a translocation between two of my chromosomes. (Be forewarned if you *Google* this horrific condition.) Like a Picasso painting, I have all of the correct chromosomes, but they are not put together properly. Fun fact: it actually shows only 45 (versus the normal 46) chromosomes on my lab results; so that is good dinner conversation.

This not only made becoming pregnant quite difficult, but it also made the actual pregnancy one of high-risk. Throughout the different visits with genetic counselors, the Chronic Villus Sampling (CVS) test, and then the following procedures, I felt a divine nudge that she would be all. She. Was. It. Henley June is the only child that I will have naturally. Thankfully my husband felt the same nudge. We were so richly blessed with the knowledge of my condition beforehand, and, well, not to sound cliché, we felt that with this knowledge came great responsibility. There are times in life when God whispers, "*you* choose, my child." And then there are other times when God proclaims, "my child, *I* have chosen."

During this time my loved ones seemed more fertile than ever. In my brokenness, bitter jealousy ensued. I, too, had visions of a bustling house full of children. I would pray these faithless feelings away. Over time the Holy Spirit convicted me that time spent comparing my story to them was a waste of my own holy moments. Yes—the loud houses of many children *were* beautiful, but my house would be as well, and in more ways than I could have *ever* imagined. At this point of conviction, I surrendered to the will of the Spirit. (That is usually the way it goes, right?)

As I lay on the operating bed in the final step of ensuring my funky chromosomes would never taint a zygote, I prayed aloud (the doctors had stepped out of the room), "God, You are here. You are here. Though there is some sadness here, *You* are here. Thank You for the chance to birth Henley. Thank You for my body doin' its miraculous thing. You called Garrett and me as co-creators, and we thank You. Thank You for Henley. Use me, Lord, use our family however *You* see fit. I know You have work for me to do. May I see and love every child at the church as one of my own, especially the Bluebonnet Children. Oh, the Bluebonnet Children! You are here, Lord, and I feel that You want me to shift my focus now on birthing their book. Lord, if I am misguided, redirect me; but yes—I need to, I *must* birth a book for the Bluebonnet Children, I—" my intercessory moment was interrupted by the doctor entering the room, and the peace of Christ filled me.

The local church has become my bustling house full of jovial, high-energy children, and Henley June feels just as much at home there as I do. She was named after the one and only poem by a Brit named William Henley who wrote of having an *unconquerable* soul, and a country singer who loved hard (what a combo, no?). Her namesake has painted the lens through which I see the children I serve, especially the Bluebonnet Children.

Just recently a fifth-grade boy from a *very* troubled home came bounding down the hall, "Miss Meg! You walked by me without giving me a hug." Disclaimer: I am not really a hugger. I'm more of a shoulder-tap-kind-of person; which this boy could care less about and gave me the biggest bear hug ever. As he hugged me, I prayed within, "Dear God, despite all odds, give him an *unconquerable* soul, may our church work *so* hard at loving him that his soil does not stand a chance at defining him."

Pray, pray, pray! Pray fervently for the Bluebonnet Children in your midst. Not only does prayer sustain *you* and your church family as you serve, but from it will bloom the most resilient and faithful disciples. Build up those Bluebonnet Children, church! Seek them out, invite them in, pray them up, and teach them to stand firm on the Truth expressed by the apostle Paul in Romans 8:31–39:

> *"What then are we to say about these things? If God is for us, who is against us? He who did not withhold his own Son, but gave him up for all of us, will he not with him also give us everything else? Who will bring any charge against God's elect? It is God who justifies. Who is to condemn? It is Christ Jesus, who died, yes, who was raised, who is at the right hand of God, who indeed intercedes for us. Who will separate us from the love of Christ? Will hardship, or distress, or persecution, or famine, or nakedness, or peril, or sword? As it is written,*
>
> *"For your sake we are being killed all day long;*
> *we are accounted as sheep to be slaughtered."*

No, in all these things we are more than conquerors through him who loved us. For I am convinced that neither death, nor life, nor angels, nor rulers, nor things present, nor things to come, nor powers, nor height, nor depth, nor anything else in all creation, will be able to separate us from the love of God in Christ Jesus our Lord."

CHAPTER 3

Biblical Bluebonnets

BLUEBONNET CHILDREN HAVE BEEN around since the dawn of time. Ever since families have been putting down roots, some of them have been planted in poor soil. We are a broken people. While we see Bluebonnet Children within the programs of our church, they can also be found in our Bibles. Their stories, we must remember, are *descriptive* as opposed to *prescriptive*. Certain scriptural scenes, though recorded, were *not* fabricated (nor blessed) by God; they are simply describing the sinful choices of others. The most bizarre descriptive texts usually speak to the cross-cultural, time-traveling adventure that is reading one's Bible. Other portions of Scripture are divinely recommended for us to "go and do likewise" (Luke 10:37). God must hate the darkness of the first as much as we do; but we must remember that in all things, God is at work for good (Romans 8:28). The stories below are heavy, but in Christ there is hope.

When did you last prepare a lesson over Jephthah from the book of Judges? This is not a very common lesson in the Children's Ministry realm, for the only "take-home point" it delivers is "how to be a bad father."[1] Jephthah's mother was a harlot and his father was well-to-do. Jephthah was sent to live with his father, where he was then despised and mistreated by his half-siblings. Jephthah's

---

1. Garland and Garland: *Flawed Families of the Bible*, 179–82.

father was silent throughout all this mistreatment. Fueled by his rage, Jephthah grew into a mighty warrior that led the Israelites into battle against Ammon. He then took a vow and sacrificed his daughter after defeating the Ammonites.

There was also King Saul's daughter, Michal, whom we meet in 1 Samuel. She fell hard for the future king of Israel, David. In a sense, he already felt like family to her due to his friendship with her brother and professional relationship with her father. Unlike the customs of the day, she proclaimed her love to David first. Sadly, it is not recorded if this love was reciprocated. What we do know is that this initiated her use as a pawn in a slew of governmental games between the two men and her brother. In time, her assertive love for David morphed into an assertive distaste. While David's fame and fortune grew, so too did her bitterness. Eventually, her poor soil of the house of Judah disintegrated.

As it goes for most Bluebonnet Children, "bitterness breeds bitterness"[2] and the abusive cycle continues. Those roots just dig deeper and deeper into poor soil with each passing generation. At least this was the case for King David's righteous daughter, Tamar. Not only does the church detest this scriptural scene, but I am certain God does as well. Her brother, Amnon and his cousin, Jonadab, created a sick scheme so that Amnon could act on his lustful feelings towards her. Amnon raped Tamar.

Out of pure hatred, Amnon tried to send Tamar away afterwards, but she fought him on this. Despite the fact that this was unlawful (in many ways), David, did nothing because of his love for Amnon. Thankfully her other brother, Absolom, took her to live with him where she lived out the rest of her days in despair and depression. Absolom shared these feelings with her until the grudge erupted into him having Amnon murdered (2 Samuel 13).

If only we were not a fallen people. If only all parents strived for the example of Elizabeth and Zechariah in the book of Luke. As proud parents of John the Baptist, they were "righteous before God, walking in all the commandments and ordinances of the Lord" (Luke 1). If only all parents in our programs viewed their role in

2. Ibid., 151.

this way. But, like the above families, some have roots grounded in *very* poor soil. We don't deny this. We face it "heart on". We choose to focus our energy on the potential that *is* the Bluebonnet Child. Despite the poor soil, her bonnets develop beautifully once showered with God's grace.

CHAPTER 4

The Bible Tells Me So

WHEN WE THINK OF the Bible, we typically think it is a book for adults by adults. However, children are referenced over 8,000 times. As the late great Christian educator Roy Zuck taught, "Biblical narratives include dozens of children. [It includes]children with Godly parents, and ungodly parents, wealthy children, poor children, rebellious children, obedient children, children with physical ailments, children with unlikely names and those with desirable names and miracle babies."[1]

We can flip to the Old Testament and read:

Deuteronomy 6:4–7

Hear, O Israel: The Lord is our God, the Lord alone. You shall love the Lord your God with all your heart, and with all your soul, and with all your might. Keep these words that I am commanding you today in your heart. Recite them to your children and talk about them when you are at home and when you are away, when you lie down and when you rise.

Or

Psalm 10:17–18

O Lord, you will hear the desire of the meek;

1. Zuck, *Precious in His Sight*, 13–15.

you will strengthen their heart, you will incline your ear

to do justice for the orphan and the oppressed,

so that those from earth may strike terror no more.

We can flip to the New Testament and read:

Mark 10:13–16

People were bringing little children to him in order that he might touch them; and the disciples spoke sternly to them. But when Jesus saw this, he was indignant and said to them, "Let the little children come to me; do not stop them; for it is to such as these that the kingdom of God belongs. Truly I tell you, whoever does not receive the kingdom of God as a little child will never enter it." And he took them up in his arms, laid his hands on them, and blessed them.

Or

Ephesians 6:1– 4

Children, obey your parents in the Lord, for this is right. "Honor your father and mother"—this is the first commandment with a promise: "so that it may be well with you and you may live long on the earth."

And, fathers, do not provoke your children to anger, but bring them up in the discipline and instruction of the Lord.

Furthermore, the presence of children in the early church is well-documented throughout Paul's writings. Though young, they were vital members of the home church movement. Stories of the entire household—including children—of Lydia, Stephen, and the Philippian jailor can be found throughout the books of Acts and 1 Corinthians.

It seems as though the prophets, apostles, and Gospel writers knew what they were talking about. They were aware of the sad fact of Bluebonnet Children, and they were even more aware of God's call on their hearts to care for them.

Jesus took this call to the next level when he redefined the term "family." Instead of an Old Testament emphasis on "clans" and the nuclear family, Jesus emphasized that we are all part of the Family of God. "God alone is the head of this divine family" and we are to love every member of this family with a selfless love.[2]

Just as it is pointed out in James 1:27:

> "Religion that is pure and undefiled before God, the Father, is this: to care for orphans and widows in their distress, and to keep oneself unstained by the world."

The book of James has always fascinated me. Unlike other letters in the Bible, this one is not addressed to a certain person, city, or congregation. Also, there is no reference to a date or time in history when this book was written. Finally, because there were four men in the New Testament with the recorded name of James, the verdict is still out on which James authored this book.

With great authority, the author is holding all Christians, regardless of city and century, accountable to "living out of true devotion, to care for the orphaned and the widows." The word "orphan" in Hebrew means "fatherless" and in Greek it means "comfortless" or "loveless". The word appears in the Bible *more* than 40 times.[3]

Whenever I think of one being in need of comfort and love, Mario comes to mind. He is a dynamic fifth grader who moves swiftly and enjoys juggling lots of tasks at once. I do not know the details, but neither of his parents are in the picture and his aunt and uncle are his guardians. For the longest time, his family operated within a "drop-off-ministry" model. They would pull up to the church at 9a.m.; Mario would jump out of the car, and then at 12:15p.m. the car would reappear to pick him up. I will never forget the one time he was cheerfully bouncing down the stairs after Sunday school saying, "Man, this church is like a hotel!" (Insert full-tooth grin). I will also be forever touched by the moment in worship when he subtly teared up during prayer time. The Holy Spirit was already at work in his life *long* before he entered our doors.

2. Garland and Garland: *Flawed Families of the Bible*, 126 and 180.
3. Zuck, *Precious in His Sight*, 13—15.

With his natural wiring, he became an excellent technical assistant for children's church. Despite the fact that this church runs for grades kindergarten through fourth, some fifth graders just cannot quit us. They serve as assistants. Mario loves the rush of responsibility. Arriving 30 minutes before the other children, he sets up the projector and screen. He pulls up the *YouTube* clip I send to myself, and has it all prepared to play when cued. As soon as 11a.m. hits, he puts on the hat of greeter and welcomes the kids into the sacred space. At the close of worship, he puts the tech equipment back in its place. Yes—the cords are always neatly coiled.

As he has faithfully served out of his gifts, Mario has grown as a significant member of the Body of Christ. A year has passed since we first met, and now both guardians and three siblings also join him *every* Sunday. This 11-year-old has built up the Kingdom! His story is one of many examples that children are *not* the church of tomorrow, they are the church of *today*. Over age 18 or not, the hope-filled message of Christ sounds the same. All are qualified to increase the Gospel's volume through study, prayer, and service. Bluebonnet Child or not, we are called to come alongside them in committed service and learning.

CHAPTER 5

Supplemental Hope

ALL OF US LIVE within varying types of social circles. These shape our views and our actions more than we realize. While some of these circles are of our choosing, others are not. I have been richly blessed by those in my professional circle. Serving on the *Big Brothers and Big Sisters Board* was a divine connection for me a few years back. The director of this fantastic organization helped me to grow in my understanding of the Bluebonnet Family; and to increase my awareness of the unique needs in our area.

I will forever treasure one of the board members. She was a police officer who handled all cases of child abuse and registered sex offenders. Both she and the director were extremely brave women. They were committed to bringing light into the darkness. I was timid at times to serve alongside them. Some of the situations were so devoid of hope. When a red flag would appear with a child or family, the three of us would pick up the phone and network until a resolution was found. This was a powerful social circle, and I feel the development of Bluebonnet Children was enhanced through some of the steps of action we took.

Throughout many fields of study, the holistic development of a child has been under the microscope. These differing fields offer us supplemental hope. One example is the theory of Russian-American psychologist, Urie Bronfenbrenner's Ecological Systems. From this structure of the environments, it is made clear why "he views the person as developing within a complex system of relationships affected by multiple levels of the surrounding environment".[1] From a child's microsystem to mesosystem, to exosystem, and all the way out to the macrosystem (which one might want to avoid during election seasons), all of these "rings of relationships" play a *huge* role in the child's overall development. The poor soil of a Bluebonnet Child's mesosystem does *not* have the final say in how they will develop as an adult; other rings can affect the child's emotional quotient (EQ), intellectual quotient (IQ), habits, problem-solving techniques, worldviews, and religious views.

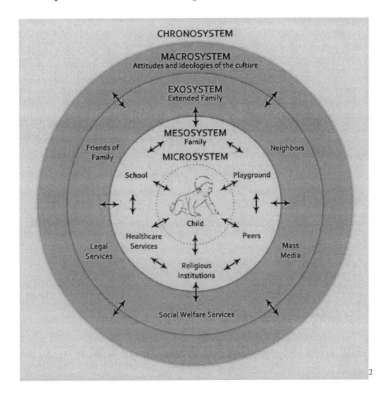

1. Berk, *Development Through the Lifecycles*, 24.

2. Graphic by Lauren Lewis

For example, a local church could easily be placed within the mesosystem of the child on this chart. Feeling the pressure yet? I do. And this pressure *is* good for the local church. It's good to carry that responsibility. It is good to not only believe that what we do matters but more importantly to actually *do* something that matters in the life of a child.

Another theory that points to hope outside of a child's home is from Russian psychologist Lev Vygotsky, whose main points are pictured in the graphic below. It is known as the sociocultural theory. In this theory, he states that a child's cultural context has a much greater shaping effect than the child's natural wiring. He argues that instead of researching the child's stages of development, those involved might focus more on the beliefs, customs, and skills of the surrounding community.[3] A child desires to emulate the thoughts and behaviors of her community as she grows into a contributing member. The *village* does, in fact, raise the child, *not* just the parents.

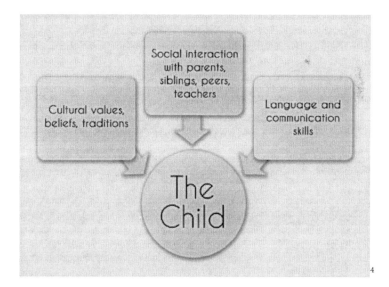

3. Berk, *Development Through the Lifecycles*, 25
4. Graphic by Lauren Lewis

From the famous *Orange* curriculum (a very popular children's ministry resource that is rooted in the home/church partnership), we know that if a child attends church on Wednesdays and Sundays, we will see him around 100 hours a year; whereas the child will be with his family around 3,000 hours (considering school and sleep).What type of difference could we possibly make in the life of a Bluebonnet Child in just 100 hours a year?

Recently I arrived home from work on a Sunday to find a 15-year-old girl leaning against the tree in our front yard. She was crying, well—bawling to be exact. Though I had known Lydia for 11 years, I had not seen her since she started high school. How did she even know where I lived? I only knew her through our church programs. She shared with me that she desperately needed to call her grandmother.

She would not stop crying. Once we got back to the church to find the number, she opened up to me. Her parents (Bluebonnet Children themselves—just longer stems) were going through a divorce. Her mother lived an hour away, and she was staying with her dad in town. Earlier that morning, he had told Lydia that he was going to sneak her out of the state. She protested, he slapped her and then she ran two miles to my house.

While she was on the phone with her mother and grandmother, I stepped out into the office hallway. Her mother's passionate voice rang through the phone, "You stay at the church. You hear me, he can't get you there. We trust the church. We've known Meg a long time, and you will be safe there." Lydia and I waited in the church for two hours for her mom to arrive. Our lunch was made of leftover wedding scraps, and we painted in the craft room. It was so good to see Lydia smile while she inhaled her food. We talked some but painted mostly. She painted me an abstract cardboard circle with pure hues and geometric shapes. It still hangs in my office.

Once her mom pulled up, I was able to share with her the helpful resources within our community. Although our church might have only seen Lydia for 100 hours a year for the past 11 years, it seems as though the impact of our ministry might easily last a lifetime.

Beautiful things happen when the church answers the call and serves Bluebonnet Children. The hard part is already done—God is already active in these kid's lives. The Holy Spirit is communicating to their hearts. Studies reveal that 15% of 4,000 people interviewed claimed that their relationship with a higher power began when they were children. Although these persons had *no* religious upbringing or training, they were able to describe their profound childhood experiences in great detail 30 to 40 years later.[5] Whew, there is hope. God's got this!

---

5. Stonehouse, *Joining Children on the Spiritual Journey*, 128.

CHAPTER 6

The Triple A Approach

WHILE THERE IS NO objective formula to best serving the Bluebonnet Child, there are certain steps we can take as we intuit our way through it! I call it the Triple A approach. No—this is not an auto club to call when your car breaks down. It is way better (and less expensive). The Triple A approach will equip you as a vessel that showers Bluebonnet Children with God's grace. This approach calls us: to be aware, to advocate, and to articulate in their lives.

"Pssst—are we allowed to bathe the infants in the kitchen sink?" I heard this as I was attempting to read a story to our preschool class. I turned to see a caretaker with the filthiest little brunette boy on her hip. The dirt and residue had been on his chubby arms for so long that a rash had emerged beneath the grime. Trying to preserve his dignity by controlling my face, I smiled, passed the book onto my assistant and joined them in the hall.

"Come again?" I said.

"He's just really dirty, and his odor is, well—you can smell it, I'm sure." She said this while gently swaying this oddly happy baby. "His bottom is caked inside of his diaper, just caked—as if it hasn't been changed in a while; so we were thinking we could bathe him real quick in the church kitchen?"

"Sure." I said, "I will call the mom and let her know. Also— slap some diaper cream on his bottom, please."

I shook my head in disbelief as she walked away. She then turned back and said, "Oh, one more thing. His lunch today is a half-eaten *Taco Bell* burrito. Can you ask the mom how she expects us to serve that to her eight-month-old?" My heart dropped. What was already an uncomfortable conversation with the mom, just got more uncomfortable.

This is what we do in children's ministry, right? Yes—we do *whatever* it takes—pray mercilessly for our kids, stay late to prep lessons, *Prezis* at board meetings, shift teammates to best honor their gifts, and, oh yeah, pretend to be unshakably bold. Whatever it takes to lead these kids closer to the healing grace of Christ—*we will do it*! Why? Because we were made to live in no other way—to serve in no other way *but* this. Why do we do it? Because we are called. We are called to serve Bluebonnet Children.

So I picked up the phone.

"Hi, Leslie, It's Meg from Kids' Day In," I said.

"Yeah," the lower-income, teen mom said over the television noise in the background.

"I hope you are well. Jeremy is doing fine. He is so happy today," I said. (Butter them up before the blow—right?)

"Yeah." She murmured again.

"I was calling because I was curious about Jeremy's bath schedule." I bravely said.

"Yeah, he gets baths," she nonchalantly replied.

"Great. Well, today his caretakers thought it would be helpful to give him an extra one due to his odor, and he seemed to have some dirt on his arms. So if it's ok with you, they are going to bathe him in the sink." Whew—I got that part out.

"Yea." She, obviously, could not care less.

"Also, I am sure your family is good in this area," my nerves were starting to get the best of me, "but, if ever you guys need help with water bills and such, our office can help with that."

"We got water." An inflection change was present in her tone.

"Sure, sure, sure, well just in case you ever need that, we are here to help you." I practically exhaled these words.

"Yeah. We're good," she shared.

"Awesome. Also, Leslie, how would you like us to feed Jeremy today?"

"I left a burrito in his bag," she said.

"Yes, we saw that. I am wondering if he might enjoy a jar of baby food better." I began to realize that she thought this was an appropriate meal for an infant.

"If you guys have some, give 'em one," she blurted.

At this point in the conversation, a rush of gumption filled my soul. I had to fight for this little guy: "Leslie, I can only image how difficult being a new mom is." [silence] "So if ever you need some extra help and support, there are these great parenting classes downtown at the *Eagle Nest*. They are so helpful," I said.

"How much do they cost?" She said with mild excitement.

"Don't worry about that. Our office could help with that if you are interested."

"Yeah," I heard over the phone. I sensed my time to exit the conversation was near. Our chat had been weighty. I needed to give her space to ponder.

"Thanks for your time, Leslie, and please call me anytime if there is any other way I can be helpful."

"Yeah," she said one last time.

In the four years that followed, I watched Leslie grow into a very caring and responsible mom. After that day, Jeremy never came to KDI in such a dirty state again. In fact, one day I had a sub, and when I returned, Leslie took me aside to tell me that my sub did not change Jeremy's diaper in a timely fashion. It was refreshing to see the concern on her face. I tried not to smile as she was complaining to me, but I was truly proud of the parent she had become. I was thankful that the Holy Spirit led me to a better understanding of Jeremy's story, led me into fighting for him, and helped me to clearly state how Christ and His church desired to support him.

With the Holy Spirit's help, we can be more aware of children's stories. We can advocate for their needs, and theologically articulate how the healing power of Christ is at work in their lives. The next three chapters will cover the individual components of this approach in more depth.

CHAPTER 7

Be Aware

TO BE TRULY AWARE is a treasure worth seeking; awareness of self, of the present moment and of others. Know that every minute is valuable and full of potential when it comes to reaching out to the Bluebonnet Child.

Before growing in our awareness of another, we must first know and love ourselves well. This is not news to you, but there is not a single parishioner who feels it is her divine vocation to help you maintain your level of self-awareness and self-management. Would not it be great if there was a committee of beloved church members whose sole purpose was to manage this? (Sign me up!) Do not get me wrong, they love you and your ministerial leadership; but taking care of you is up *to you*. Nurture your soul, so God can create soul-nurturing moments through you.

In our attempts to be self-aware, we naturally discover and hopefully honor how God wired us. There are many great resources for this, and one that has recently enhanced our staff's life is the Servant By Design (also known as Process Communication Model) assessment.[1] Founded by the clinical psychologist, Dr. Taibi Kahler in the 1980s, this unique tool has stretched out of the secular business world and is currently required by all clergy in some United Methodist conferences. Not only did Kahler set out

---

1. Learn more at http://servantsbydesign.com

to teach that each person communicates differently, but also that each person has a "different/predictable pattern of distress when his needs are not met positively".[2] From this, we learn to trust the gifts and to respect the limits of ourselves and others on the team. Each person on your team has a unique set of skills, life experiences, and a natural wiring that could bless a Bluebonnet Child; but the first step to serving is being self-aware. "Ya wanna know what sets highly influential people apart?" Education guru, Todd Whitaker says, "They are aware of how they came off to others."

Along with being self-aware, one must also be aware of how the Holy Spirit is moving in his life. While we will unpack this further in another chapter, the key is prayer. Hold it at the forefront of your mind that the child who takes the *most* patience is in the *most* need of your ministry; and an arsenal full of that much patience *only* comes from a routine of prayer. As we tread on the poor soil in which a Bluebonnet Child is planted, we must be *prayerfully* in tune with the Holy Spirit. Or as William Carrey put it, "Prayer—secret, fervent, believing prayer—lies at the root of all personal godliness."

This divine dialogue sustains us as we seek to be more aware of the Bluebonnet Child's story, and believe you me, some pages can be pretty dark. Once we are self-aware and aware of the "Holy Spirit's hums" (one of my boss's favorite lines), it becomes quite easy to be fully aware and present in each moment. When you practice that level of awareness, keep an eye out for the signs of abuse, some of which are listed below.[3]

SYMPTOMS OF CHILD ABUSE

Children who have experienced child abuse may demonstrate any of the following signs.

2. Pauley et al., *Here's How To Reach Me*, 2–3.

3. The Kansas Department of Children and Families. *A Guide to Reporting Child Abuse and Neglect*

Symptoms of Physical Abuse

- Demonstrating behavioral extremes, including very aggressive or demanding conduct
- Appearing frightened of the parent or caretaker
- Being full of rage, passive or withdrawn
- Being apprehensive when other children cry
- Verbally reporting abuse
- Being extremely hyperactive, distractible or irritable
- Demonstrating disorganized thinking, self-injuries or suicidal behavior
- Running away from home or engaging in illegal behavior, such as drug abuse, gang activity or cult activity
- Displaying severe depression, flashbacks (including hallucinatory experiences) and dissociative disorders
- Sudden changes in behavior
- Child starts wetting or soiling clothing or bed
- Sleep problems, including nightmares
- Cannot recall how injuries occurred or offers an inconsistent explanation

Symptoms of Sexual Abuse

- Verbally reporting abuse
- Seductive behavior, advanced sexual knowledge for the child's age,
- Promiscuity
- Expressing fear of a particular person or place
- Excessive masturbation
- Sexually abusing another child

- Delinquency, runaway or truancy
- Self-injurious behaviors, suicide attempts
- Extreme fear of being touched;
- Unwilling to submit to physical examination
- Poor peer relationships
- Repeated urinary infections
- Pregnancies or STDs
- Difficulties sitting down

Symptoms of Emotional Abuse

Common Indicators within the Parent/Child Relationship

- Rejecting or belittling the child
- Ignoring the child (taking little or no interest in the child)
- Terrorizing the child by blaming the child for things for which the child has no control
- Isolating the child (cutting the child off from normal social experiences)
- Repeatedly giving the child contradictory messages that leave the child confused
- Using an inconsistent, unpredictable, erratic and threatening style of discipline

Common Behavioral Indicators of the Child

- Daytime anxiety and unrealistic fears
- Sleep problems, nightmares

- Biting, rocking, head-banging or thumb sucking in an older child
- Substance abuse
- Fire starting
- Loss of interest
- Sudden grade changes
- Changes in behavior, personality

Being aware of these signs not only leads us to advocate for this child (more to come on this), but it helps us to understand the implications poor soil will have for the learning environment. In any teaching space, there are external and internal factors that could potentially prevent the child from learning at her best. In my opinion, abuse can take the form of both. The first are those that are physical distractions outside of one's person, say if a child's new sweater is itchy or there is an electric drill buzzing next door. The latter, internal factors, are emotionally-based.

As neuroscientist, Eric Jensen, writes, "although all of us acknowledge that we have emotions, few of us realize that they are not the cards on the table *but* the table itself. Our emotions are the framework of our day."[4] The primal spark of "fight or flight" is housed at the base of the brain in the amygdala; it is *literally* the foundation of the mind.[5] If this spark is ignited too often (which it is for Bluebonnet Children), the other functions of the brain (rationalizing, creativity, memory) shut down (*They shut down!*).This is not a matter of a bad mood or a good mood. Cognitively speaking, it is *impossible* for the brain to perform well if one is living out of fear and uncertainty. The best teachers have a heightened sense of both external and internal factors and they adjust their lesson and the teaching and worship space accordingly.

Another external factor that should be considered is a child's socio-economic class. This paints a different worldview for each person. While we might be more aware of it in lower class families,

4. Jensen, *Teaching with the Brain in Mind*, 80.

5. Ibid., 97

poor soil can be found in *any* class. I was once guilty of judging the impoverished families of our community for how they ran their families, and I am so thankful for the incident that gave me a change of heart.

As soon as the strap hit my shoulder I knew something was not right. Heart racing, I unbuckled my bag only to find that my wallet had been stolen. Stolen? Yes—stolen. I was heart-broken; it was most likely pocketed by a person who came to our office seeking shelter, funds, or food.

The community meal was the next day at my church and, unlike previous shifts, I was not feeling good about this one. My heart was bitter. Needless to say, the disappearance of my wallet gave me a resentful filter through which I viewed the entire evening. My usual common courtesies of small talk or topping off waters were non-existent.

Despite my sullen mindset, I remained faithful to my volunteer hours. The following week was Christmas, and each family would receive a gift from us. With my prickly attitude and low expectations, I began lining up 20 plus bags of groceries.

The fake holiday cheer of mine quickly faded with the first person who fought me on the "one-per-household" rule. It also did not help my morale when families sent different children through the line to get an extra bag. But I remained faithful. I showed up and served.

My infant daughter joined me at the next weekly meal. I wore her in a carrier. She and I weaved through tables giving refills and taking trays. Similar to before, I was not emotionally present until a voice shook me out of myself. "How old is your baby?" I turned around to see a round-faced, brunette in her mid-20s with a messy ponytail and pastel sweats. She was surrounded by a flock of children.

Our paths had crossed before, but the extent of our conversation was based on her preferred amount of gravy.

"One," I said.

"She walkin' yet?"

"Yes. On Christmas Day, she just decided to take off," I replied.

After sharing a chuckle, she did something unexpected. She went around the table and shared the early milestones of all of her children. Sharing at great length, she spared no detail. Her cup overflowed with pride and love. Her memory far surpassed mine, and I only had one child. Prior to this moment I had wrongfully doubted her competence as a mother. In fact, since the wallet situation, I had been viewing all of the guests as potential thieves who could not be trusted.

Suddenly, I was ashamed of my thoughts and suspicions. As I walked back into the kitchen, the Holy Spirit humbled me. I realized that while my lens was temporarily tarnished, God's perspective is always grace-filled. God loved her and me in the same unconditional way. Regardless of social-class, God sees through a filter of love. Instantaneously, my negative lens was wiped clean, and my bitter dehumanizing thoughts vanished.

Awareness of one another's story is key as we serve others in Christian love. Even though grace is God's gift to all social classes, each person brings a different set of values and perspectives to the table. Since Bluebonnet Children can be planted in any socioeconomic class, it does nothing but enhance our ministry if we are intentional in our understanding of these differences and opportunities.

One leading expert on this topic is Ruby Payne. While I do not know her personally, she holds a very special place in my heart. My mother was enthralled with her work while she was completing her Masters of Education Degree. Her work has been monumental in the world of education and has influenced numerous community initiatives that are eradicating poverty (not an overstatement). In Payne's book, *Bridges out of Poverty; a Framework for Understanding Poverty*, she clearly articulates the unwritten parameters by which the impoverished, the middle class and the wealthy move through the world. Payne teaches that;

> *"Each individual is shaped by environment to a certain extent. If you are in an environment where resources are scarce, then the decision making is different. How you spend your time is different, and in poverty it is often spent*

on survival. Because there is less margin for error, decision making becomes concerned with survival. Allostatic load increases in the brain, and this in turn generates survival responses. When your resources are stable (as they generally are in middle class), then you have the time to plan. When you have an abundance of resources and time to plan (as people in wealth usually do), then the decision making is influenced much more by exploration, choices, and aesthetic value.[6]

The differences she is writing about are listed in the following table.[7]

6. DeVol, Philip E., et al., *Bridges Out of Poverty*, 42–43.

7. *Source: Excerpted from* Bridges Out of Poverty: Strategies for Professionals and Communities (2009. *DeVol, Dreussie-Smith, Payne.* ©2009 *by aha! Process, Inc.) Reprinted with permission.*

Hidden Rules of Class

	POVERTY	MIDDLE CLASS	WEALTH
POSSESSIONS	People.	Things.	One-of-a-kind objects, legacies, pedigrees.
MONEY	To be used, spent.	To be managed.	To be conserved, invested.
PERSONALITY	Is for entertainment. Sense of humor is highly valued.	Is for acquisition and stability. Achievement is highly valued.	Is for connections. Financial, political, social connections are highly valued. social connections are highly valued.
SOCIAL EMPHASIS	Social inclusion of people he/she likes.	Emphasis is on self-governance and self-sufficiency.	Emphasis is on social exclusion.
FOOD	Key question: Did you have enough? Quantity important.	Key question: Did you like it? Quality important.	Key question: Was it presented well? Presentation important.
CLOTHING	Clothing valued for individual style and expression of personality.	Clothing valued for its quality and acceptance into norm of middle class. Label important.	Clothing valued for its artistic sense and expression. Designer important.
TIME	Present most important. Decisions made for moment based on feelings or survival.	Future most important. Decisions made against future ramifications.	Traditions and history most important. Decisions made on basis of decorum.
EDUCATION	Valued and revered as abstract but not as reality.	Crucial for climbing success ladder and making money.	Necessary tradition for making and maintaining connections.
DESTINY	Believes in fate. Cannot do much to mitigate chance.	Believes in choice. Can change future with good choices now.	Noblesse oblige.

	POVERTY	MIDDLE CLASS	WEALTH
LANGUAGE	Casual register. Language is about survival.	Formal register. Language is about negotiation	Formal register. Language is about networking.
FAMILY STRUCTURE	Tends to be matriarchal.	Tends to be patriarchal.	Depends on who has money.
WORLD VIEW	Sees world in terms of local setting.	Sees world in terms of national setting.	Sees world in terms of international view.
LOVE	Love and acceptance conditional, based upon whether individual is liked.	Love and acceptance conditional and based largely upon achievement.	Love and acceptance conditional and related to social standing and connections.
DRIVING FORCES	Survival, relationships, entertainment.	Work, achievement.	Financial, political, social connections.
HUMOR	About people and sex.	About situations.	About social faux pas.

With this chart as a tool in comprehending my experience at our community meal, offering mercy naturally takes less effort. My wallet was (most likely) stolen by one who sincerely believed that he had no real control over how his life turned out. Like cards, the lives of the impoverished (so they believe) were dealt to them and *choice* plays no role in their circumstance. Unlike other socioeconomic classes that revere the concept of personal responsibility, whoever took my teal Liz Claiborne wallet believed that the rest of the world owed him something. No judgment here—it is what it is.

Furthermore, since persons in extreme poverty operate out of a "survival mode"(in which all decisions are based on temporary feelings) it makes sense that many parents deemed it "moral" to send their kids through the grocery gift line under false pretense. When people's main goal is feeding their family, the black and white rules of the surrounding culture fade to gray. Political connection? Personal achievement? Nope—the driving force here is to simply live. Wake up tomorrow morning? Mission accomplished.

When people are operating out of survival mode, they are also unable to plan ahead or even envision the future. All basic needs must be met first. Sadly this is not the case for those who are in poverty. We know this from Sir Maslow's Hierarchy of Needs. Basic needs must precede all psychological needs and needs of self-fulfillment.[8] It should not be surprising to us that our meal guests are not rushing to worship with us on Sunday morning. How can we expect them to give any thought to the spiritual trajectory of their lives while they are not even sure from where their next meal will come? And for those of us who serve in Children and Family ministry, what does partnering with a parent from this family look like?

Grappling with questions such as these will equip us as a Bluebonnet Child's supplemental family and in time, Christ will reveal the answers. As partners with Him in the Gospel, He is counting on us to become aware; aware of self, aware of His holy hums (through prayer), and aware of the internal and external factors of each child's story. May our awareness move us towards the actions described on the pages to come.

A REVIEW OF WHAT IT LOOKS LIKE TO BE AWARE OF A BLUEBONNET CHILD'S STORY

- Do your best to become self-aware. This naturally honors how God wired you. There are many great resources for this, and one that has recently enhanced our staff's life is the Servant By Design assessment.[9] In any teaching opportunity, strive to trust your gifts (talents) and to respect your limits.

- Along with being self-aware, you must also be aware of how the Holy Spirit is moving in your life. While we will unpack this further in another chapter, the key is prayer. Hold it at the forefront of your mind that the child who takes the *most*

---

8. Cherry, *The Everything Psychology Book,* 11–12
9. Learn more at http://servantsbydesign.com/ .

patience is in the *most* need of your ministry; and an arsenal full of that much patience *only* comes from a routine of prayer

- This divine dialogue sustains us as we seek to be more aware of the Bluebonnet Child's story, and believe you me, some pages can be pretty dark. There might come a time when Christ calls you act once you have become aware of some signs of abuse.

- The best members of a Children and Family Ministry Team are those that have a heightened awareness of the internal (emotional) and external (outside of oneself) factors of each child's story in each learning opportunity. As Jensen teaches, "although all of us acknowledge that we have emotions, few of us realize that they are not the cards on the table *but* the table itself. Our emotions are the framework of our day."[10] Due to the anatomical makeup of the brain, a Bluebonnet Child's mind *cannot* function at its fullest potential if he or she is living out of constant fear or uncertainty.

- Another internal factor to consider for each student is his or her socio-economic class. This paints a different worldview for each child in your care and will also come into play as you seek to partner with his or her parents.

---

10. Jensen, *Teaching with the Brain in Mind*, 80.

Chapter 8

Advocate

THERE IS A VERY popular book called *Eat This, Not That: Thousands of Simple Food Swaps that Can Save you 10, 20, 30 Pounds*" by David ZinkZenko. In this book ZinkZenko compares different entrees of varying chain restaurants. Studies are presented to show the surprising caloric difference between a burger from McDonald's and Burger King. Are you craving a breakfast sandwich? Then (to the disbelief of everyone) eat at McDonald's, not Starbucks.

As I look back at serving Bluebonnet Children, there are many ministerial moments I wish I could have "done this" and "not that." Even though I was aware of the family's story and was aware *enough* to begin advocating for the child, the steps I took were not the most helpful. Bluebonnet Children long for those outside of the home to champion for them. They desire and require one who not only *believes* they can be healed from their poor soil, but who *fights* for it as well. A cheerleader, if you will, who is consistently on their side, rooting loudly until their needs are met is the role of the Body of Christ, but what does this look like? The following scenarios are examples of better and worse ways to advocate for Bluebonnet Children, including one which demonstrates the difficulty of advocacy.

DO THIS

Our church office is usually hopping with *Helping Hand* interviews where folks can receive financial assistance for utilities or other basic needs. As the families pass my office, they are sometimes rambunctious—no, dysfunctional, in how they speak to their children. I have begun providing small snacks and a box of blocks as soon as I hear them coming. I greet them with a smile and some entertainment options. Empathizing with their worldview (kudos, Payne!), I am able to engage in a conversation with the parents. This not only helps the family feel welcome during a vulnerable and slightly awkward moment, but it frees up the parent to focus on the interview. Furthermore, another smiling face (in this case, mine) in the life of a Bluebonnet Child is *always* a good thing.

NOT THAT

As very loud, and impolite families walked by my office to go to their Helping Hand interview, I closed my door before they saw me. Shameful—I know. My heart was re-broken every time I heard how they addressed their children. Once they had left the building, I would often rush to the binder of the interviewee's contact information and stash their name in my mind. I would then bring up the name to my social worker contacts to see if this family was already on some mythical "watch-list" of abusive families, which actually exists only in my mind.

DO THIS

I presented a need for more Bibles at a Church Leadership Council meeting for the afterschool program that had a growing amount of "unchurched" children. I (thankfully) had all the details lined up and ready. So when a saintly, retired lawyer *unexpectedly* whipped out his checkbook and asked, "how much do you need?" I was prepared to accept the gift on behalf of the kids. This same saint would continue to advocate when he paid for the therapy sessions of two very dear Bluebonnet Children in our church family.

NOT THAT

I once wasted fifteen minutes of my life trying to convince a non-convincible parent that it was "right" to provide Bibles to children who were not members of our church. They "had not earned it" (her words, not mine) by being faithful in their attendance of Sunday worship.

WHAT TO DO?

While shopping at the grocery store, I overheard a six-year-old girl crying uncontrollably in the book aisle. As my husband and I followed the sounds, we found a grandmother repeatedly beating the young girl's hand.

We kept walking, but only for a few minutes. I then turned to him and said, "I have to go back." Shaking in my boots, I walked back to the books. "Hi," I said, "everything okay here?" (As if I had any ounce of authority to ask such a question.)

"No!" the grandmother growled, as she continued to beat the child's hand, which was now beet red.

"She won't stop asking for candy!" she barked.

My blood began to boil. "Oh, I see." I placed my hand on the small girl's shoulder. "I can only imagine how hard it is to be a parent in moments like this."

She hit her hand again, and the girl cried harder. "Yeah—she knows better."

Seeing that our conversation was going nowhere, I shifted my attention to the little girl. "I'm sorry we don't always get what we want. Maybe next time you can get some candy?" She stared at me with wet, blonde strands covering her eyes. To the grandmother, it was as if I was not even there. I only hoped that my presence meant something to the girl. After realizing I was not being helpful, I walked away in quiet tears and loud prayers.

I do not know if I did the right thing in this situation. I wish I would have been bolder. I replay this memory over and over again, wondering how I could have moved differently. There was not a single person in the store that hadn't heard her cries and moans. Many even saw her continually (*continually!*) getting hit. Should I have followed her and recorded her license plate number? Did the employees at this store have any obligation to intervene and take action? Did someone step in after me and do something to help this little girl? I hope so!

I would honestly say that out of the three steps involved in the Triple A Approach, advocating is *truly* the most challenging. It offers *many* more roadblocks than our attempts in awareness and articulation. However, in Christ there is hope! By the power of the Holy Spirit, let us explore our options as mighty advocates for the Bluebonnet Children in our midst.

ADVOCATING WITH THE PARENTS: BLUEBONNET CHILDREN WITH LONGER STEMS

In this line of work, we are trained that parents are the primary faith nurturers and our role is to partner with them in helping their children take their first steps of faith. While a partnership does occur in our attempts to advocate for Bluebonnet Children, it does look slightly different. As I shared before, 99.9% of the time, Bluebonnet Children were brought into this world by Bluebonnet Children with longer stems. In our service to these children, we will have to learn how to work with their parents—some more than others. You are the judge of the level of interaction you will have with certain parents. I can recall moments that I intentionally did not share a child's poor choice with the parents out of fear of what would await that child at home.

While relationships with the parents we serve might vary in appearance, there are some general rules that can be applied to all.

One leading voice on this subject is Todd Whitaker.[1] I was blessed to learn from him at an educational conference recently. And my approach to working with parents has shifted greatly thanks to his concepts. His guidance is not only simple (not to be confused with easy), but also immediately applicable.

There were about 20 of us packed into a high school classroom in my hometown of Mabank, Texas. Todd bobbed and weaved through the cluster of chairs as he shared. The first challenge was to keep our perspective in check. For example, if you are dealing with an arduous parent, know that she communicates in a harsh way to *everyone*. It is not about you (it has nothing to do with you). But it is the *only* way she knows how to express herself. Most likely a Bluebonnet Child herself, she is truly living, loving, and communicating to the best of her capabilities. This is not an acceptable excuse, and it doesn't make it right. But that is how she truly is. We *must* wrap our minds around this awareness before diving into a conversation with this type of parent.

Once our mentality is in the proper place, we can "sidle up" to this parent before the conversation begins. Instead of facing them head on, we can stand at their side in a less confrontational way. Knowing that their fury is *not* about us, we can let them do their own emotional work while we stick to the facts. We are non-reactive, we gather information in note form (where they can see), and above all else, we treat them as if they are not harsh. This is a very powerful point in Whittaker's teachings. Those who act in such an abrasive or argumentative way do not know what to do when another responds to them in a calm and collected fashion.

Whittaker challenges us to *continually* seek these difficult parents out and to treat them as if they are as calm and collected as anyone else. Go a step further and treat them the same as you do your most faithful and responsible parents. Offer them all of the same opportunities to thrive. Invite them to Bible Studies with other parents and parenting events at Eagle Nest.[2] Introduce them to other parents at pick-up and drop-off time and 'like' their social

1. Whittaker, Todd: *Dealing with Difficult Parents*, 49—62
2. Learn more at http://www.eaglenestinc.org/

media updates. Expect the same from them as your most reliable parents, i.e those who volunteer, provide snacks and commit to a timely pick-up. Always (*always!*) welcome them with kindness (even though you might think they are the least capable parent you have ever laid eyes on). This level of discomfort will slowly alter the steps they take with you, which will enhance your ministry as an advocate to a Bluebonnet Child.

KEEP THEM SAFE!

While there may be varying levels of concern for children's safety (depending on the parent), I am convinced that 'safe' is nearly synonymous to "successful" in our Children and Family Ministry programs. The value of security is a top priority for *most* parents. One step in assuring the welfare of all is to create a Safety Policy for your church.

Now, before the operational and tactical side of this compels you to hurriedly turn the page—hear me out. There is a very helpful tool I can offer you to help make this a reality for your church family. It's called BeaDisciple.com.[3] This is a digital hub for Christian education with professional wisdom at extremely reasonable prices. You will find a course which uses Joy Thornburg Melton's text, *Safe Sanctuaries*, to walk your team through creating your own Safety Policy. The course blessed us with a consultant that held our hand every step of the way. With focus groups, data collection, and then the actual writing (and rewriting and rewriting) of the policy, this intimidating task turned out to be a lot more manageable. The course also guides your team in ensuring *your* policy meets the unique needs of your church's programs. Here is my church's policy, as an example.

---

3. Learn more at http://www.beadisciple.com/.

FUMC CHILDREN'S SAFETY POLICY

The "Six Month Involvement" Rule

This requires all volunteers who work with children to be active participants of FUMC Winfield for at least six months before they are allowed in any position involving contact with children. During this six-month period they are highly encouraged to serve as an assistant in a program. This rule does not apply to paid staff, due to KDI and nursery workers mostly being undergraduate students at neighboring colleges.

Interviewed, Screened, and Trained

All children's ministry team volunteers, along with paid KDI and nursery staff will be required to fill out an application, undergo an interview, background check, and Boundary Awareness Training which is offered through the Great Plains Conference of the United Methodist Church in the fall.

The "Two Adult Rule"

This requires no fewer than two adults present at all times during a church sponsored program, event, or ministry involving children. Risk will be reduced more if the two adults are unrelated. In desperate circumstances, a volunteer under the age of eighteen, yet inline with the "Five-Years" rule, can serve as one of these "adults". Furthermore, in the nursery, one of these adults can be serving on a volunteer basis whereas the other is a paid position. Abusers thrive on secrecy, isolation, and their ability to manipulate victims. When abusers know they will not be left alone, they lose interest in working with children.

The "Five-Years Older" Rule

Leaders must be a minimum of five years older than the children they are working with. This rule does not apply to the High School ministry program.

Volunteers Under the Age of 18 Must Be an Assistant to an Older Adult

People under the age of 18 cannot be expected to have developed the maturity and judgment that is needed to fully respond to young children. With this said, people under the age of 18 can only assist with an older adult. This rule does not apply to nursery workers, who can be as young as 16 to serve.

Windows or Dutch Doors in all Classrooms

A window or Dutch style door removes the opportunity for secrecy and isolation. A Dutch style (half) door offers protection against children wandering outside the classroom and allows for full visual access. Any classroom doors without windows should remain open at all times.

Open-Door Counseling

At any counseling session with children, the doors on the room used should remain open for the entire session, ideally when others are nearby, even though not in listening distance. Counseling sessions conducted behind closed doors are a breeding ground for false allegations of abuse. Closed doors make it easy for a child abuser.

First Aid/CPR Training

Providing first aid and CPR training on an annual basis for all church workers with children is a basic step to assuring the safety of children. Having workers who are prepared to deal with bumps, bruises, and scrapes with competency goes a long way toward building the confidence of children and parents involved in the children's ministry.

Advance Notice to Parents

A basic rule with children's ministry is to always give parents advance notice and full information regarding the event(s) in which their children will participate. Before the event, parents must give written permission for their child to participate. Churches are protected insofar as the parent has been informed of the event. Advance information gives a guideline to parents about scheduling and allows parent and child to decide if the event and its content are suitable for their participation. It also demonstrates that the church has planned thoroughly to provide the safest experience.

Participation Covenant for All Participants and Leaders

A written covenant of participation should be developed and provided to all leaders and participants in children's ministry which they agree to: (1) take part in the ministry, (2) give their best efforts to the ministry, (3) respect the other participants, (4) treat others as well as they would wish to be treated. Such a covenant is especially useful for establishing the onset of behavior standards expected by everyone. It is also an important reminder for leaders that abusive behavior toward the children will not be tolerated.

It has been several years now since our policy was created, and it has been so refreshing to have this foundation as we strive to protect the safety of our children, adult volunteers, and the overall integrity of our program. A supplemental tool that has helped us along the way (and that is required by our denominational conference) is www.Safegatherings.com.[4] It makes screening and training for abuse prevention *beyond* simple for our KidMin team. Safe Gatherings certifications are only good for three years. Our Office Administrator maintains our certification records.

Having a solid safety policy in place sends the message, "We love you with the love of the Lord, and we are going to work our tails off to provide you with a safe, nurturing church family, filled with loving and equipped Christ-like mentors to guide you as you grow in your faith. Despite the poor soil to which you may return, here at [insert your church's name] you will learn that God's grace has the final say in how you blossom in life."

ARM THEM WITH TOOLS TO TAKE HOME

Not only can we do our best to assure their safety while they are within our care, but we can also fight for their needs if we equip them to care for their own needs. "Mindfulness" is a huge buzz-word right now in both the secular and spiritual teaching arenas. Although this practice is far from cutting-edge, new affirming research has rebirthed it. This therapeutic technique equips one to fully concentrate on the present moment. In peacefully noticing and accepting one's thoughts and feelings, he can take ownership of these and guard them from the actions of others in the past or future. Some of the major benefits of this mental training include

---

4. Learn more at https://safegatherings.com.

boosting the immune system, lowering the risk of heart disease, and decreasing one's symptoms of depression.[5]

Although, mindfulness exercises can take the form of sculpting a symbol of one's day out of playdough or rediscovering one's grounded-ness while laying on the floor with soft music, one of the original forms was a lesser kinesthetic version—prayer. As one of London's leading voices in mental health, *The Mind & Soul Organization* teaches;

> *"Within the Bible there is an implicit theology of attention and awareness. Jesus goes off very early in the morning to a solitary place to pray, which is an act of sustained attention (Mark 1:35). Peter and the disciples hunt him down and interrupt him, trying to distract him with what the crowd wants. Jesus switches his (and their) attention back to what really matters and says, 'Let us go somewhere else—to the nearby villages—so that I can preach there also. That is why I have come' (Mark 1:38)."[6]*

Not only is Jesus seen prioritizing stillness in the New Testament, but so are our Hebrew ancestors in the Old Testament. The prophet Elijah was striving to hear the voice of God, and while mistakenly thinking it would be heard in an earthquake or a fire, it was found in a still small voice in 1 Kings 19. As a compliment to the Biblical emphasis on solitude, neuroscientists and psychologists offer many helpful resources on the subject as well. One that I have recently found very helpful is "The Whole Brain Child" by Dan Siegel and Tina Payne Bryson. Here, mindfulness is taught to combat the "flight or fight" feeling that many children experience while in fearful or uncertain situations. Even a child with extreme behavioral issues has been found to behave better after a moment of mindfulness than he would have after a moment of conventional punishment.

One school in Baltimore has replaced visits to the principal's office with a mindfulness room and behavior and academic success

---

5. Wax, "A Mindfulness Guide for the Frazzled." 57.

6. Lambert, "A Christian Perspective on Attention, Awareness, and Mindfulness."

has never been better. The school is located in a very low-income area with a high crime rate. Many of the children struggle to feel a sense of security and love. Upon entering the mindfulness room, a trained facilitator leads a child through a breathing exercise. Once this is complete, the two begin to explore the emotions that surrounded the behavioral issue. In time the student's visits to the mindfulness room decrease, and they begin utilizing these helpful methods on their own wherever they may be.[7]

This is such a mighty tool for children to take with them from your programs. While they cannot control the *actions* of others, students can learn to own their emotions and take control of their *reactions*. In pausing for a moment of solitude, they can tap into the sense of peace, strength and affirmation that only the Holy Spirit who dwells within can provide. While the concept of mindfulness could have been placed anywhere within the Triple A Approach (be aware, advocate, and articulate), the fact that it arms kids to fight for their own needs outside of your church programs puts it in this chapter.

One of my most affirming moments in ministry came from a mindfulness exercise, during a fifth grade after-school program. I loved this group of nine preteens so much, but if these students had attended the school in Baltimore, they would have spent *many* hours in the mindfulness room. This was quite a challenging bunch. Each Wednesday I would go home and research how to present a more engaging lesson. In my research I came across mindfulness exercises.

One day after their routine time of snacking and mingling in the church courtyard, I invited them up to the teaching space. We reviewed last week's lesson and I shared with them how proud I was of them. I pointed out that I sensed some distracting feelings were being brought into our space and that I wanted to help them take control of those so they could get the most out of their time in the program. I then showed them a short and powerful video called "Just Breathe" by Julie Bayer-Salzman and Josh Salzman

7. Folgelson, "Baltimore School Deals with Conflict by Sending kids to the Mindful Moments Room Instead of the Principal's' Office."

(*Youtube* it!). This amazing clip is made up of children teaching the practice of mindfulness to adults. It is beautiful.

After the video, I invited them to find a comfortable place in the room to lie down on their backs far from their friends. I dimmed the lights, played some soft spa-like music, and walked them through what is known as a grounding exercise. This involves focusing on one's breath—the rise and fall of the abdomen along with tightening and loosening different muscle groups. Knowing the energetic dynamics of this group, I only allowed three minutes for this. I then led them through an echo prayer. While still lying comfortably, they repeated after me. At this point, the Holy Spirit filled my mouth with different words than were on my script. The prayer that came out was one of forgiveness for those whose presence or absence had caused us pain. We then prayed to see ourselves as God does—a strong, smart, and loved tween. At this point, my eyes were closed and I heard (what I assumed was long overdue) snickering.

As I opened my eyes, I saw six of the nine students crying. The other three were respectfully remaining present, while the room was enveloped with a slew of emotions. I was speechless from shock. My prayer was over, but I felt the Spirit nudging me in a different direction. I asked the kids to give a thumbs up if they desired more time. They all did. For the next five (yes—five!) minutes, they continued to breath, to cry, and to experience the palpable presence that is the hug of God; while I, awestruck, subtly sobbed like a baby in a chair off to the side. I was no longer needed for the remainder of the exercise.

When five minutes were up, I left the lights dim and invited them back together as a group. I had not planned on a time of sharing, but once again, the Holy Spirit had different plans. In a gentle way I invited anyone who so desired to share their thoughts of this moments. This then opened the floodgates to the most vulnerable and deep moment of sharing. Some shared stories of divorced or incarcerated parents. Others shared of the lesser sadness of GPA-inflicted stress and peer pressure. One boy cried with his entire body for his mom who had abandoned him when he was four. I tear up now just at the memory. To my utter amazement, every student was respectful and comforting as the others shared, and what was meant to be a three-minute activity stretched into 30 minutes.

In the weeks that followed, the youth requested more moments like this. One time when tensions were rising during a team-building activity, Mariah jumped up on a chair, turned off the lights and belted at the top of her lungs, "*You all need to center your selves! We are not communicating well!*" We did *many* more mindfulness exercises and in time they all grew in awareness and ownership of their own emotions and reactions—despite the poor choices of those in their lives. More importantly, they learned how to tap into the healing voice of God which resides within. Arming Bluebonnet Children with spiritual disciplines such as these is a *mighty* way to advocate for them.

A CRUSADER FOR CHILDREN'S WORSHIP

Children of abusive or neglectful homes lack the necessary resources for a healthy life. With this said, it is most likely the case that opportunities to foster one's faith are also absent. It is for this reason that intentional moments of worship for Bluebonnet Children are a must. There seems to be three schools of thought on the issue of worship for children. One values the child being *physically* present the entire worship service so corporate worship may be modeled by the Body of Christ. Another prefers a more age-appropriate option away from the sanctuary to ensure that the child is *mentally* present. The third group of parents are those who, for one reason or another, have no preferences on worship.

The first two stem from holy places and value the overall spiritual health of the child. And the third calls us to step up our game, because these kids might not be getting it anywhere else. At my church, we surveyed our parents to determine their preferences and hopes regarding children in worship, and to no surprise we learned we were serving families with preferences all over the spectrum. The end result was a lovely compromise.

KEEP IT SHORT:

The CC (Children's Church) worship experience only lasts the length of the sermon and the prayer. In our church that is around 25 minutes. Plus, on communion Sundays (#highchurch), CC is much shorter to assure that the children are back to receive the sacrament with their fellow church family members.

KEEP IT FRESH:

To best meet the needs of our families and volunteers, we do not offer CC on holiday weekends. Furthermore, this will be the first time in six years that we are offering it during the summer. Much-needed breaks like these "keeps the lettuce fresh" as my senior pastor says. It allows time for the children to miss CC and for the leaders to take a break so they are geared up to work with kids.

KEEP IT THEMATIC:

As a member of the Worship Planning Team, I assure that CC is in line with the day's sermon, and I get ideas from the worship planning team. Though children and adults are momentarily worshipping in separate spaces, we are worshipping together. In the worship guide, the parents are guided with "On the Drive Home" questions that can springboard them into a conversation with their child over the morning.

KEEP IT DIFFERENT:

Children's Church is not Sunday school. Just as we adults expect something different from the sanctuary than from our small group—the same is true for children. While we pour biblical content into the minds of our kids at Sunday school, CC is a sacred space to pour their hearts out to God. At worship, as Robert Webber teaches, "We remember, anticipate, and celebrate the work of the Lord in our lives." CC can be exploratory, yet structured, energetic, yet solemn. It can be a full and also margin-filled time where children are equipped to turn up the volume of the Holy Spirit in their lives.

With the help of Marlene Lefever's work, *Learning Styles*, our CC template assures that the unique way in which each child's brain is wired is honored. As children first arrive we arrange ourselves in a circle on the floor. Once we are all comfortable, we experience the following.

WELCOME AND EXPECTATIONS THE STAGE IS SET FOR A SACRED TIME.

The next 25 minutes is unlike any other time of their week. They need a reminder to be respectful as they and their friends strive to hear God's voice. Our three expectations are to: listen, try with their whole hearts, and have fun.

"HOOK" QUESTION/ACTIVITY:

Our kids are asked to turn to the partner next to them and to discuss a question that immediately engages their imagination with the scripture. Once they share with their partner, two or three kids can share aloud with the whole group. For example, if the scripture was Jesus walking on water in Matthew 14, a hook question could be, "when was the last time you did something that at first was scary?" This discussion could be followed by a game to reinforce the concept.

ECHO PRAYER:

The prayer that we created is designed to intentionally build up the children with sound theology. It is called an echo prayer because a different child is chosen to lead the prayer each time, while the others repeat (echo) each part. There are also a few hand motions splashed in towards the end to help engage their memory of the prayer. After a semester, the majority of kids have it memorized. Our hope is that the prayer can become as easy as breathing, a centering piece, if you will, before we enter into worship.

KID VOLUNTEER:

Good morning God. (echo) Thank you for making us.(echo)
Good morning Jesus. (echo) Thank you for healing us. (echo)
Good morning Holy Spirit. (echo) Thank you for guiding us.(echo)
We are ready to listen (echo) with our hearts to what you say. (echo)
Your voice is much louder (echo) within this special place. (echo)
Quiet down my brain (echo) and slow down my feet. (echo)
I came to worship, to hear you (echo) come now, here's a seat (echo).

At the end of the prayer, the adult volunteer guides the children to close their eyes and imagine what they would tell Jesus if He were to be sitting right next to them. A quiet moment is left at this time (say, 20 seconds) so the children can think or whisper their response.

WORSHIP THROUGH SONG & DANCE:

The following sing-along DVDs are very helpful: *Deep Blue* by Cokesbury, *Sing-Along by* FaithWeaver, *Play & Worship*, and *Celebration Place; Sing & Praise*.

BOOK:

This is the portion of the worship experience where the scriptural content is presented. A helpful text in creatively presenting this is Aaron Reynolds's *The Fabulous Reinvention of Sunday School*. This might include the storyteller being in costume and telling of how Jesus walked on water while he or she actually sits inside a cardboard boat. Perhaps blue butcher paper covers the floor where the children are sitting.

LOOK:

If the Book portion was presented in a more energetic, large group fashion, than we aim to make the Look piece more introspective. This part of the worship goes into how the scriptural content is applied in the 21st century. An example of this might be passing out wave-shaped sheets of paper and fun pens and inviting the kids to spread out all over the room and chew on such questions such as, "why do you think Peter started to sink?, Is it important to the story that the wind and the waves listened to Jesus?, Why is it sometimes difficult to trust in Jesus?" We play some soft music and place a large three-minute sand-timer upfront to guide their solo work.

TOOK:

We bring it all home with a weekly benediction that is based on the possibilities. What would happen if this scripture was applied this week? A way to make this scripture relevant would be to make care-packages for our recent high school graduates as they face a scary, but necessary, time. These packages could be thematically water-based, and have cards that read, "Trust in Jesus—Stay Afloat in College," or other kid-friendly lines.

The best news about Children's Church is that the most important work is already done. The Holy Spirit is communicating to these young disciples. The only work we have to do is create a sacred space that enables the children to tune in to the conversation.

Easter Praise!

My 15-month-old-daughter illustrates this in the above picture (after shoving her way to the front of the group just to be closer to the music and then dancing her heart out!). If we prayerfully expect the Spirit to move in their little hearts, nothing will stand in the way of their *big* transformation.

A REVIEW OF WHAT IT LOOKS LIKE TO ADVOCATE FOR A BLUEBONNET CHILD

- Bluebonnet Children long for those outside of the home to champion for them. They desire and require one who not only *believes* they can be healed from their poor soil, but who *fights* for it as well. The role of the Body of Christ is as a cheerleader, if you will, who is consistently on their side, rooting loudly until their needs are met.

- While a partnership with Bluebonnet Parents might be more difficult than with other parents, it still is necessary. Whittaker challenges us to *continually* seek out these difficult parents and to treat them if they are not difficult. Go a step further and treat them the same as you do your most faithful and responsible parents. Offer them all of the same opportunities to thrive. Expect the same from them as your most reliable parents. This level of discomfort will slowly alter the steps they take with you, which will enhance your ministry as an advocate to a Bluebonnet Child.

- Although there may be varying levels of concern for children's safety (depending on the parent), I am convinced that "safe" is nearly synonymous to "successful" in Children and Family Ministry Programs. The value of security is a top priority for *most* parents. One step in assuring the welfare of all is to create a Safety Policy for your church. Create one now to protect your volunteers, children, and the overall reputation of your ministerial programs.

- Arming Bluebonnet Children with spiritual disciplines such as prayerful mindfulness is a mighty way to advocate for them. Tools like these help them grow in their awareness and ownership of their emotions and reactions—despite the poor choices of those in their lives. More importantly, they learn how to tap into the healing voice of God which resides within.

- Fight for Bluebonnet Children by assuring they have intentional worship opportunities in which they learn in age-appropriate ways while also worshiping with the *entire* Body of Christ. These children most likely are not getting these sacred moments anywhere else, so let us get to it!

CHAPTER 9

Articulate

THE THIRD AND FINAL step in the Triple A Approach calls for us to theologically articulate the grace-filled hope and new life that awaits these Bluebonnet Children in Christ. Conversational tools can be helpful in this endeavor. Such tools encourage proper listening, while also meeting the needs of more tactile learners. For almost a decade now I have used the same, palm-size painted stone as a talk-rock for varying ages during prayer time. (Yes—I hear you, if it were smaller, it would be deemed a "prayer pebble.") The stone is gray, and it was given to me by a camper at Camp Quinipet in Shelter Island, New York, where I served as a chaplain. Like many stones on the Peconic Bay, this one is deep gray, and the waters have sanded it down to its soft, lovely state. The camper painted the top of it with different colored stripes. It is smooth on the bottom, but highly textured on the top.

As a talk-rock, the kids hold it and pass it as they share their prayers. While they sit in a circle, they know that the only person who can speak is the one holding the stone. All the other children must aim to be good listeners. It beautifully sets up prayer time. At the end, I close us in prayer holding the same rock. This stone is more than special to me, it is sacred. It holds a subtle power after so many young disciples have held it while tuning into the Holy Spirit.

Over the years, I have heard some charming, prayerful moments. Pre-schooler, Hazel once lifted up this prayer, "Dear, God.

My mom says, 'Hazel, you don't got a choice.' But God, all I want is more choices, so if you could give me some—that would be great. Also, thank you for bacon." And a kindergartener once stated his entire prayer in the voice of a *Transformer*. Praise for *Pokemon-Go*, and strength to unlock the next level occurs often in all the grades.

While these moments are pure and quite humorous, there have been many more moments of holy depth. Transcendent moments of praying with children flood my memories. Many times during our pre-school lunch, I have had to hide my tears. One of my most beloved Bluebonnet Children, Ellis, had a speech impediment. For five years he would offer up the most long-winded prayers; his eyes tightly shut, the stone tightly clenched. No one could understand a *single* word, but his passion left the room (of other young children) silent in attention. The only word that was clearly articulated was "Amen!" I looked forward to his prayers each week.

There have been times during prayer that I have cringed a bit, due to some heretical undertones. I have heard fearful prayers toward God (since God *killed* Jesus), "Please don't do it again, God." Prayers *against* those who are homosexual have also been offered from these young ones, "Help us to not talk to them", one fifth grade boy said. And materialistic lamentations have been prayed more than one can imagine.

You do not need me to tell you that the "littlest of these" require mentors in the faith to prayerfully articulate how the Holy Spirit is moving in and around them (while also *kindly* correcting the false teachings they bring with them). While children can sense that something different is occurring as they enter our church doors (hopefully), they lack the language to claim and capitalize on it. Not to mention the fact that some holy hums could easily be drowned out by the noise of the world. As the creator of *Godly Play*, Jerome Berryman states, "Religious language gives words, narrative, and parables that help us to make sense of our experiences with God, to come to know God better and to make meaning of what we experience and learn in all of life."[1]

---

1. Stonehouse, *Joining Children on the Spiritual Journey*, 170.

A LAST-MINUTE LAMENTATION

I will never forget Holy Week of 2014. Our church family had lost one of our own to cancer, and his granddaughter was in our after-school program. With a numb expression on her third-grade face, she sat in the circle awaiting the Easter story. The funeral had just been a few days ago. As I looked down at my legal pad, I immediately realized that the opening question of describing the sights, sounds, and feelings of a funeral was *not* going to fly. If I was not careful, this teaching moment could potentially paint an incorrect picture of the church for Jenny.

As you have surely done before, I prayerfully made a last-minute change to my plan and prayed for the best. I was careful not to minimize, nor sugarcoat, the importance of Christ's sacrifice. A brief recap, or an overview would be a gentle transition into the darkness that is the cross. Using our *Action Bibles*, the passages they had studied that semester came to light again. We spoke of how *the entire* Bible has been building up to this point. God wanted to be close to His creation and to bring it back to Him, so He sent His Son to live *with* us—as *one of us*. The kids shared ways that Jesus teaches us to have a close friendship with God. The discussion led us to the fact that some of God's creation will choose *not* to seek after Him, which brought us to the trial and the cross.

I panned the circle to assure Jenny was doing okay then continued treading lightly, "More important than the cross, was the empty tomb." [quick page turn to new pic] "With the empty tomb, we see that there is *nothing* that will keep us from God. Anything that stands in the way of our friendship with Christ—even death—will be defeated; and through the power of the cross we too become conquerors in Christ. That is how *very* much God loves us and desires to bring His creation back to Him."

"How big was the tomb they buried Jesus in?" Sonja asked. Before I could even get a response out, Jenny dropped her face into her hands and began sobbing.

The vibe I was getting from her since she walked in was *not* to draw attention to her, and I respected that. Now, the attention was on her, and only her. Not sure of my next move, I whispered a prayer. While wanting to comfort her, I wanted to do it in a way that respected her space. "Funerals are so hard, guys."

I mustered up the courage to continue, "No matter whose funeral it is—they are hard. Jesus' funeral was different than other funerals, though—"

I was interrupted by a young, overzealous theologian, "Because He was *God's* son."

"Yes." I smiled and went on, "It was different because his funeral *and* resurrection were used to teach us that nothing could keep us from a forever friendship with Christ—not even death. Jesus did come back to *earth* on Easter Sunday. This is *very* different than our humanly funerals. We will not see our loved ones again *on earth.*"

Jenny wiped her tears away and sniffled. I resumed, "But—we *will* see them again. In a different way, we will see them again. We will see them through every story and memory shared, and in a special place that Jesus has prepared for us—heaven. Just like God was at work through the cross and empty tomb, He is also at work in all the funerals of His children even though it may not feel like it. While it may seem dark and sad during a funeral, joy is coming and we can say thank you to Jesus for that."

Once the session was over, I asked Jenny if I could speak to her in private. I could tell that she *still* did not want to talk about it. I gave her the church-appropriate-side-hug, and said, "I am so *very* sorry about your Grandfather. And I also apologize if any part of this lesson was difficult for you today."

I saw the faintest smile appear on her face.

"Thank you." She said.

"We love you and your family so much at this church, and we pray you will feel the comfort of a giant hug from Jesus right now." I said.

"Thanks." She turned and walked down the hall.

IS YOUR TEAM EQUIPPED TO ARTICULATE?

These moments, during which we intuitively, and soundly articulate how the Holy Spirit is moving are *monumental* in the spiritual development of a child. Your teammates must not only be able to teach biblically sound lessons, but they must also do their best to read the kids as well (remember in chapter seven?).

It scares me to think of what would have happened had I not prayerfully altered the lesson. A "good" lesson could have been presented without me ever altering it on-the-spot. How would Jenny have felt about organized religion if I would have not sensed the internal and external factors at play for her as a learner? What would her take-away have been if I was not equipped to offer up a theologically sound lesson on a whim? These. Moments. Matter. And we need to do everything in our power to assure that teammates are equipped with sound theology, and a high (enough) emotional quotient to "read the room".

Equipping a team happens in many ways, but one that we found works well for us is small group book studies. We have studied everything from Henri Nouwen to Sarah Bessey to Todd Whitaker. Since most of our children's programs overlap with worship, Sunday school or other opportunities for the team to nurture their own spiritual health, it is imperative that we set aside additional time for this. How can we be expected to offer up spiritual nourishment, if we ourselves are not spiritually nourished?

These small groups are made of six to eight persons and are quite formative. Pondering deep thoughts with those who are in the trenches of ministry with you is a true gift. It is not only a gift to me personally, but it has also provided a bonding experience for our team. These groups have also had impromptu brainstorming sessions. Prayer is also a key part of our time together.

We pray for each other's families, our world, and of course, the kids and parents we serve. The more we pray, the louder the Holy Spirit's voice is in our lives. And *this* is critical as we aim to articulate theologically-sound and Spirit-filled lessons for the Bluebonnet Child, because *our* strength will fail to sustain us. As

Romans 8:11 teaches, "The same Spirit of God who raised Jesus from the dead lives in *you*." The sooner we surrender to the work of the Spirit, the sooner personality clashes, misplaced priorities, and any other sign of brokenness lose their power.

Theology and worldviews are tested and sharpened in these groups. As those aiming to teach well, this time polishes the articulation of our faith. Differences in our doctrinal thoughts may reveal themselves, but with education and time we learn that our dogmatic beliefs are the same. We are committed to one another in Christian love. We have "entered a fellowship", as the mighty missionary, E. Stanley Jones said, and "sometimes we will agree to differ, always we will resolve to love, and unite to serve."

In spite of our differences, we aim to hold proactive conversations. At times we serve as each other's soundboard. Other times, we might offer mere encouragement or evaluative discussion. One helpful tool for crafting purposeful conversations is Stanley & Clinton's *Connecting: The Mentoring Relationships You Need to Succeed In Life*. The following guide from the work is taped inside each person's book in our small group.[2]

TYPES OF SHARING

- Encouragement: We will point out how we see God working in this situation. We will share hope.

- Soundboard: We will listen well. Our listening will be focused. We will share provocative feedback and will add objectivity to ideas. Questions are good in this type of sharing.

- Major Evaluation: We will readily point out inconsistencies in thought and viewpoint and test ideas for soundness.

- Specific Advice: We will give specific advice to a specific situation by sharing the possible outcomes but we will leave the final decision-making to the sharer.

- Linking: We will link the sharer to the needed resources.

2. Clinton and Stanley: *Connecting*, 95–96

This helpful guide is to ensure the "sharer" receives what is expected and needed from the "listeners". It can also draw out more clarity if a tense moment arises. I have witnessed *way* too many awkward moments when the sharer is hoping for a mere "soundboard". But the pack of listeners is barking back "major evaluations" or "specific advice". These moments in small groups can be (and have been) uncomfortable for some. I have the same amount of pity for both parties in these cases. Deep listening and formative conversations can take time and practice, and this handy sheet is a simple step in the right direction.

Once our loving commitment to each other is in place, we see past our differences and set a standard for our discussions, we are ready to dive into *who* we are when we teach and work with children.

WHAT GREAT TEACHERS DO DIFFERENTLY

Fans blow as the kids enter the classroom. A candle is aflame on the center of the table, which is adorned with a red table cloth. The seating chart has been designed based on the personalities of the group. Each chair faces a Bible, pencil and a language scramble as they arrive. The downloaded wind sound effect surrounds the space. It is Pentecost and you are beyond prepared. This is rare and you are excited to teach.

The opening activity goes swimmingly, and then Rodney and Chad begin testing the fan blades to see how quickly they can cut the pencils. This of course distracts the rest. What do you do? Some of the best prepared, most passionately presented lesson plans are sadly squelched by a teacher's lack of classroom management skills, self-awareness, and self-control.

The book, *What Great Teachers Do Differently*[3] by Whitaker is for moments like these. It is not about curriculum or instructional theory, but about who we are as teachers and how we view the children we serve. While it would be ideal to send our entire children's

---

3. Whittaker, *What Great Teachers Do Differently*.

ministry team to Bethel Seminary to earn an master's in Children and Family ministry—this book is a close second. Whitaker believes that *all* teachers can go from good to great; regardless of their talents or years of experience. This quick read will equip you as a Children's Pastor in nurturing your volunteers towards a higher standard of teaching the best news in the world—the Good News.

Todd Whitaker has written dozens of books on similar subjects, consults with 50+ schools every year, and has spent countless hours in research as a teacher and principal. While some of his thoughts may echo Bruce Wilkinson's work, he offers something special to Children's Pastors. Similar to a school principle, we need to equip and encourage not only children, but our volunteer team and the parents with which we partner. We daily wear lots of hats, and Whitaker gets that.

Like you, I have read several books on effectively equipping our teaching team, and a surprising amount of this was comprised of concepts on classroom dynamics that I have grappled to articulate and address for years. Whitaker challenges us to "Base every decision on the best people." While some of us might have been trained to "teach to the middle," where the majority of the students cluster, he proposes we set the bar high and hold all accountable to reaching it. This is truly helpful in the realm of Children and Family Ministry, because we want to welcome all children into the church. The Wyatts from unhealthy families who never behave, and their parents who "do not do church," and the Cynthias who had all 66 books of the Bible memorized by the age of four, and whose parents serve on every church committee. Both deserve a safe and high-quality space to grow spiritually.

Cynthia's parents need to know that her CFM program is safe, biblically sound, and led by a well-trained team. Wyatt's parents need to know that we love him too much for him to misbehave, and they might need some extra hand-holding as they enter into the community of faith. Both kids should be held to the same standard so as to assure their growth as disciples. Meeting the needs of all types of families, and holding proactive conversations with parents can be grueling, but Whittaker walks his readers through these times in very manageable ways.

Another sneak peek into this treasure of a text is the challenge to ask yourself before any decision, "Who is the most comfortable?". He writes, "If Mr. Negativity dominates the meeting with carping criticism, the best teachers will be uncomfortable". Do we want our best, most capable, driven, faithful volunteers (you can see their faces, cannot you?) to be uncomfortable?

Imagine with me, if you will, that a conflict arises among your teaching team. This is when Whitaker gets raw and real. As you work toward the resolution, remember that, "discomfort leads to change". If you do not wish for the "Great Teacher's" mentality or work ethic to change, you better be real careful to not make her feel uncomfortable with your chosen strategy. His personal stories on this issue are brilliant and respectful.

He writes of a team meeting where he moved his podium after everyone had chosen their seats to make the "Complainer's Club" which usually sat in the back of the room to the front row. Who do you think was uncomfortable in this situation? The persons that needed to be momentarily uncomfortable in order to move toward their full potential. The scary part of this chapter is that if we unintentionally make the "Great Teachers" on our team uncomfortable in our attempts to reach the "Negative Nancys" things can go quite the opposite direction. Yikes. You have been warned.

Once your team has taken the steps to polish their teaching game, they can truly articulate how the Holy Spirit is moving in the life of a Bluebonnet Child. This occurs by praying with/for them, sharing Biblical stories of forgiveness and healing, and undergirding each piece of your Children and Family Ministry Program with *unshakably* sound theology that will follow these children long into adulthood.

NARRATE THE SACREDNESS OF LIFE

While striving to articulate sound theology and the ways of the Spirit, we could easily overlook a pre-existing piece that is quite helpful in this endeavor. I imagine your church already has some form of faith milestones set in place for the children. These are crucial in our articulation attempts, and I have recently been convicted of this as a new parent.

"Now we are opening the door. After this we will get in the car. Mommy is buckling up while Daddy gets your snack-snack." My newborn daughter stared back at me through her car-seat mirror. Dialogue such as this had become all too common in our household. Our Parents as First Teachers educator had recently taught us the importance of narrating life for her as it occurred. This would assist in vocabulary development and assure her comfort in new places. Though she could feel, hear and see her world, she did not come equipped with the words to describe her experience.

In a sense, our role as the Body of Christ is similar—especially in Children and Family ministry. In our attempts to articulate, our programs can help turn up the Holy Spirit's volume within our Children and Family Ministry programs; it is pertinent that we narrate the sacred scenes of life.

One way to accomplish this is through milestones. While we are on a trajectory toward Christian perfection, we must pause along the way to acknowledge and celebrate the work that God has done. God is not through with us yet, but we have definitely been refined since we first met Jesus. When milestones are grounded in sound theology, infused with the Holy Spirit, and presented by the Family of God, they morph into something nearly sacramental. They serve as an outward sign of an inward change.

Holy pauses like kindergarten and third-grade bible presentations, the *big* fifth-grade service project, or confirmation jubilantly articulate what God has done in the life of a child—and equips her for what He has yet to do.

DETERMINED DESPITE ALL EYE-ROLLS

There is a Bluebonnet Child named Peter who has been part of our church family since he was born. He is currently a pre-teen. His father is incarcerated, his mother is not in the picture and his

Grandparents are his legal guardians. For a whole year, he attended Children's Church and did nothing but sit in the back of the room with a scowl on his face. I would probably scowl too if I were him. With his arms folded and shoulders slumped, he would occasionally roll his eyes if anyone acknowledged his presence, which I often did. At the end of worship every Sunday, I would give him the biggest (church-appropriate-off-to-the-side) hug and proclaim my utter happiness that he joined us today. This was always accompanied by an eye-roll. And a slight smile. This exchange went on for a year.

Then something miraculous happened. Peter invited a friend to church. His voice echoed down the hall as they ralked (ran-walked) from the sanctuary to the fellowship hall. He was practically yelling with excitement as he bragged about Children's Church to his friend. He clearly articulated the exact worship-flow from memory. As we arrived, the jubilation continued to erupt. He joined us in our worship circle (for the first time) and said the *entire* centering prayer *from memory*. He sang every song and danced his heart out. After each song he would turn to his friend and say, "Ah, man! Now this one's my favorite!" A giant grin never left his face. "Come back next week," he said to his friend, "Yep—we do this every week. I never miss it."

Stay in it. Stay faithful. Know what fickle feelings to ignore— it is not about you. It is about *who* Christ is calling you to be in the life of a Bluebonnet Child. Strive to be in tune with the Holy Spirit; infuse your programs with sound theology; and teach your tail off through age-appropriate and multi-sensory ways. Even if all you receive is an eye-roll, they are *desperate* for your *hope-filled* articulation of how God is at work in their lives. We have a story to tell to the nations! Tell. It. Boldly.

A REVIEW OF WHAT IT LOOKS LIKE TO ARTICULATE HOW THE HOLY SPIRIT IS MOVING IN THE LIFE OF A BLUEBONNET CHILD

- You do not need me to tell you that the "littlest of these" require mentors in the faith to prayerfully articulate how the Holy Spirit is moving in and around them (while also *kindly* correcting the false teachings they bring with them). While children can sense that something different is occurring as they enter our church doors (hopefully), they lack the language to claim and to capitalize on it. Not to mention the fact that some holy hums could easily be drowned out by the noise of the world. As the creator of *Godly Play*, Jerome Berryman states, "Religious language gives words, narrative, and parables that help us to make sense of our experiences with God, to come to know God better and to make meaning of what we experience and learn in all of life."[4]

- Moments in which we intuitively, and soundly articulate how the Holy Spirit is moving are *monumental* in the spiritual development of a child. Your teammates must not only be able to teach biblically sound lessons, but they must also do their best to read the children as well.

- Equipping a team happens in many ways, but one that we found works well for us is small group book studies. Here our team prays and studies together. Since most of our children's programs overlap with worship, Sunday school or other opportunities for the team to nurture their own spiritual health, it is imperative that we set aside additional time for this. How can we be expected to offer up spiritual nourishment, if we ourselves are not spiritually nourished?

- One way the local church can narrate the sacredness of life for Bluebonnet Children is through milestones. While we are on a trajectory toward Christian perfection, we must pause

---

4. Stonehouse, *Joining Children on the Spiritual Journey*, 170.

along the way to acknowledge and celebrate the work God has done. Some helpful milestones are: Bible presentations, acolyting, or the fifth-grade mission trip.

CHAPTER 10

Stories of Promise

THREE GENUINE STORIES OF hope run through my mind in my attempts to serve Bluebonnet Children. Whenever doubt slips in regarding the effectiveness of our children's programs, I appreciate the convicting nudge of these true tales. The persons below were deeply rooted in *very* poor soil as children, but thanks to the grace of Christ poured on by the supplemental family of faith, their poor soil did *not* have the final say in how they blossomed. As you read, seek out any evidence of the Triple A Approach. Who was aware of their story? Did someone step up as their advocate? How was the work of the Holy Spirit articulated in their lives?

The year was 2008, and I was fresh at my real-world job. It was fall, and a few of our staff headed to Nashville to a Youth Specialties Conference. This was such an inspirational and informative conference. I will always cherish the talk from Louie Giglio. He spoke of an extremely musical child in his youth group just north of London. This teen did not have it easy. His father took his own life when he was seven and his mother remarried a man who was abusive toward the family. This led to an extreme amount of misplaced guilt and shame on the boy.

During these tragic events this Bluebonnet Child found great respite in his faith and music. Louie took him under his wing; and in the church he found comfort. "Things got very dark there in my teenage years," Matt recalls, "but again, by the grace of God, I decided to trust Him and trust that He was in control. Even though I couldn't understand anything He was doing, just trusting that He was watching over me. I think I can trace a lot of what I do now, the songwriting and all of it, to those key moments."[1] Louie would take him to ecclesial meetings, and he would bring the house down with his mighty riffs and melodies.

His gifts led him to great success—many Dove and Grammy awards. And thanks to the healing role that Louie and others in his faith community played, his melodious ministry has strengthened the faith of others as well.

His "Songs in the Night" speaks to the stormy days that Bluebonnet Children experience far too often. "In the daylight, anyone can sing a song. When everything's going great in your life, it's a lot easier to bring a song of worship, but can you still sing to God in the dark times? I think of it like an evergreen tree. The time when you find out whether a tree's evergreen or not is in the winter. The way you find out what kind of worshiper you are is in the storms of life."[2] This famous Bluebonnet Child is Matt Redman.

Back on the other side of the Atlantic, another Bluebonnet Child's roots were being planted. Emerging from an extremely poor unmarried couple in Mississippi, she was left for her grandmother to raise. Her grandmother was a devout Christian who made church a regular part of their routine. At the age of two, this child addressed the entire congregation about the miracle of the empty tomb. Bible verses were memorized in her house before nursery rhymes. She was reading before she was three and skipped kindergarten and then second grade due to her gifted mind and grandmother's dedicated love.

During her middle and late adolescent years, she bounced back and forth between her mother's and father's houses which were in different states. Her mother lived in a very dangerous and impoverished neighborhood and worked long hours. While living

1. Toomer, "Matt Redman on Fatherhood, faith and Unbroken Faith" *https://www.guideposts.org.*

2. Ibid.

with her mom, trusted men in the family repeatedly took advantage of this young woman. This type of hurt does not set one up well for making good choices. Her mother sent her back for good to live with her father due to "bad behavior" as a teen.

Her father was her saving grace. Out of love for her he set extremely high standards for her performance in school. He blessed her with books, guidance, and a trusted daily routine. Moreover, he lived in a much safer neighborhood. She grew into an excellent student who was also highly successful in her extracurricular activities. A speech contest landed her a full ride to college, and by the time she was only 19, she was offered a radio job by CBS.[3]

This Bluebonnet Child grew into the highest paid entertainer in the *world*. More importantly, very few can compete with the amount of funds that she gives to charities. The Angel Network, O Ambassadors, and The Dream Academy all annually receive generous donations from her. Furthermore, she has started three different foundations that carry her name. One offers grants to nonprofits that support educational and leadership development. The other runs the Leadership Academy for Girls in South Africa; and the third is a newer one that champions for those in poverty on a global scale.[4]

This Bluebonnet Child's story of resilience is one to be shared, and it has been shared on the 25 year run of her talk show. Not only was it shared, but it has truly helped *millions* of others find peace despite their own stories. Regardless of how "theologically liberal" one might find Oprah Winfrey, the Christian faith made an impact on her life. Evidence of life-giving healing can be seen through her *steadfast* commitment to serving others. Who are we to say that Christ is not quietly and independently at work in the lives of those who believe slightly differently than we do?

To bookend this lovely rule-of-three, our final story of promise is also about a contemporary Christian artist. Hailing from Texas, this singer was born to a highly abusive father. Similar to so many Bluebonnet Children, his grandmother revealed the healing

3. "The Biography of Oprah Winfrey"

4. Frazer, "Charities of Oprah Winfrey".

grace of Christ to him through classic hymns. When he reached high school, his father was diagnosed with cancer. This tragedy morphed his father into a very godly man, and the abuse stopped.

His father's death inspired the son's band's first number one hit, "I Can Only Imagine." His childhood had left many scars. The singer's personal narrative was one of his father's choices being *his* fault. While seeing a grief counselor (after another member of his family passed away) he was given the challenge of, "looking at [your] own son, Charlie, instead in order to know what you would've been like in a healthy family and a God-like environment."[5]

It was at this time that Bart Millard (lead singer of *MercyMe*), began pondering what he would say to his eight-year-old self and the song "Dear Younger Me" was born. While writing this song was an extremely heartrending process, he felt as though he had shaken off the dirt of his childhood, and had also helped *many* others to do the same. The therapeutic melody below truly massages the soul and is *full* of promise. May it bless you and the Bluebonnet Children in your ministry.

Dear Younger Me *by Mercy Me*

Dear younger me
Where do I start
If I could tell you everything that I have learned so far
Then you could be
One step ahead
Of all the painful memories still running thru my head
I wonder how much different things would be
Dear younger me,

Dear younger me
I cannot decide

5. Ong, Czarina. "Why Dear Younger Me is the Hardest Song they Ever Had to Write."

Do I give some speech about how to get the most out of your life
Or do I go deep
And try to change
The choices that you'll make cuz they're choices that made me
Even though I love this crazy life
Sometimes I wish it was a smoother ride
Dear younger me, dear younger me

If I knew then what I know now
Condemnation would've had no power
My joy my pain would've never been my worth
If I knew then what I know now
Would've not been hard to figure out
What I would've changed if I had heard

Dear younger me
It's not your fault
You were never meant to carry this beyond the cross
Dear younger me

You are holy
You are righteous
You are one of the redeemed
Set apart a brand new heart
You are free indeed

Every mountain every valley
Thru each heartache you will see
Every moment brings you closer
To who you were meant to be
Dear younger me, dear younger me[6]

---

6. Millard, Bart. *Dear, Younger Me*

CHAPTER 11

Apocalyptic Assurance

WHEN I BECAME A parent, most 2a.m.s would find me watching television, and one show I fell in love with was "You, Me and the Apocalypse". A meteor is heading toward earth and all life will be destroyed in two days. Along with this horrendous news, the lead character, Jamie, has some other reasons to be upset. His wife, Laylah, was a spy who left him, and after 30 years, his mother just informed him that he is adopted; his biological parents abandoned him as an infant and his biological mother has passed away

Seeing that there is no hope, he decides to donate his body to science. His sacrifice will provide a drug for his mom that will enable her to survive the meteor strike.

As he is heading into the medical lab to make this grand sacrifice, his bio-dad, Father Jude and colleague, Sister Celine, stop him because (spoiler alert!) Jamie has an estranged seven-year-old daughter. And then his mom, well, let's just say *nothing* can keep her from protecting Jamie upon discovering his plan. She rushes to find him which leads to the scene below.

"YOU, ME AND THE APOCALYPSE" EPISODE 6[1]

[2]

(Mom, Jude, and Sister Celine, and Dave storms toward lab doors, where they are stopped by guards.)

MOM:

Excuse me, my boy is in there, and I'm getting him.

GUARD:

Not without an appointment, love.

Sorry.

MOM:

Oh, I see.

You want a tumble, do you? Is that what you're after? Come on, then!

(Mom begins to tackle the guards.)

OTHER GUARD:

Get off! Get off!

(In the distance, Jamie is seen heading toward the operating table.)

1. Hollands, Iain. "You, Me and the Apocalypse; Home Sweet Home".
2. By Source (WP:NFCC#4), Fair use, https://en.wikipedia.org/w/index.php?curid=48119407.

JUDE:
Jamie! Wait!—Don't go in there—Jamie!

SISTER CELINE:
Jamie, please.

SCIENTIST:
We're very busy.

JUDE:
Jamie, you have a daughter.

JAMIE:
What are you talking about?

SISTER CELINE:
We met Layla a few days ago.

JUDE:
And I know that it's complicated between you.

JAMIE:
Yeah, just a bit.
I wonder who the father is
Thanks for depressing me even more.

SISTER CELINE:
The little girl, she drew this.
She said this is her father that he works in a bank.
She drew you.

(She hands him a drawing of two parents and a child.)

And look, she wrote where she lives.
You can find her.

JAMIE:

I can't handle this right now.

JUDE:

Jamie, I understand.

You hate me because I ran away.

How is going in that room any different? Is that what you want?
To be like me?

*(The main lab doors crash open, revealing all of the guards lying on the
floor as Jamie's Mom triumphantly marches in to find her son.)*

MOM:

Jamie! Jamie! Jamie!

(She spots him on the second floor mezzanine.)

Get down here right now.
I said right now, young man!

(Jamie does not budge.)

Right, I'll count to three.
One, two—

JAMIE:

Mum, I'm 30 years old.

MOM:

I'm doing the talking now, Sunshine.
What the h*#l do you think you're doing?
Do you think I want some drug to survive?
Do you think I even want to survive without you?
You are loved, Jamie.
I want you to feel how I feel.
If there's a chance that this girl is yours,

then you go and find her.

You put all this Layla crap behind you

and you jump in with both feet.

And you pour every part of you into being her dad.

Your time, your energy, your love.

You pour it all in until you don't

even know where you end and she begins.

And you hope that'll be enough.

That they'll be happy.

And that you never, ever have

to see your daughter in a place like this.

Now.

I got fish fingers for tea.[3]

(She turns and exits. All others, including Jamie, soon follow.)

Who will fight for the Bluebonnet Children even when it gets challenging? Who will seek them out and bring them home where are they safe? Who will march into dark places and shout, "You are loved, and I want you to feel it!"?

Christ is counting on you! Christ is counting on you to nurture a Bluebonnet Child with the healing waters of His grace.

3. Hollands, Iain. "You, Me and the Apocalypse; Home Sweet Home".

CHAPTER 12

Follow the Call, Make a Call

WHILE TRAVELING DOWN THE road of the Triple A Approach, one might come to a fork. Here he will "see something" and then have the tough choice of "saying something". One route might appear more comfortable for the moment, but the other could offer a child hope for a *lifetime*. Part of following Christ's call to serve Bluebonnet Children could mean making a call to the Department for Children and Families.

It is tempting to leave this dark work up to the "professionals." It is common to think someone else will say something. It is convenient to turn the other way, pray and feel that will suffice. Do not give in. Do not lower that standard. Do not miss out on an opportunity. Even if the call does not go as you expected—you *still* made a difference.

Patrick was a preteen when he joined me in the hall right outside of my office. I had known him since he was a toddler. I timidly dialed while he cried. I shared with the caseworker that his parents had never married. His father had left him with an ex-girlfriend and fled the state. In the house where Patrick was staying, there were drugs. Furthermore, the ex-girlfriend desired to take Patrick out-of-state to meet up with the dad. Patrick no longer wanted to live with either.

When the caseworker requested more proof for such a claim, I asked Patrick to join us on speaker phone. According to the well-intentioned woman on the line, this was not enough evidence. Patrick shared story after story of abandonment, emotional abuse, and occasional physical abuse. He spoke of many pill bottles and smaller cigarette-looking-thingies. These seemed of little importance to her. She wanted the names of *both* of his parents, their address, and who had custody. This information could not be found in the tense moment. I was beginning to lose hope in "the system." Patrick was taken out-of-state that night. My phone call seemed irrelevant. The child I called about and anyone related to him was no longer in *my* state. Sadness overwhelmed me.

Then something miraculous happened. Due to the high volume of calls they had received from others in our faith community, the office of Child Protective Services called me the next day for more information. They then called the office in South Carolina, where Patrick would be attending school. A social-worker was sent to Patrick's father's house (yes—states away!). Not too long after, Patrick went to live with a much more stable aunt.

If only I knew then what I know now, this attempt to help would have looked a little different. I would have called agencies like Childhelp (1–800–4-A-Child) who are skilled in providing crisis assistance, even if *all* the caller has is a simple suspicion. As we forge onward, here is a helpful guide from the Kansas Department of Children and Families[1] to assist us as we dial.

Q: What type of information should a report contain?

A: Both mandated reporters and concerned citizens (that is you.) should attempt to include the following information:

- The name and address of the child, the child's parents, or other individuals responsible for the child's care
- The child's location

---

1. The Kansas Department of Children and Families. *A Guide to Reporting Child Abuse and Neglect.*

- The child's condition, including the nature and extent of the child's injury

- Whether the alleged perpetrator has access to the child

- Any other information that the reporter believes might be helpful in showing the cause of the injuries or the extent to which the child might be in danger.

Q: Will the identity of the reporter be disclosed once a report is made?

A: Kansas law provides the identity of the reporter may not be disclosed to the child's parents, persons having legal responsibility for the child or to such persons' legal representatives. The protection is not absolute, however. If a case is heard in court or if a DCF finding is appealed and heard in a DCF administrative hearing, there is a possibility the identity of a reporter will be discovered.

Q: How quickly are reports of suspected child abuse or neglect investigated?

A: Based on the age of the child, nature of the allegation, continued access of the perpetrator to the child, and other factors, Kansas Protection Report Center social workers determine the response time assignment for the report. If the Kansas Protection Report Center social worker determines a child is in imminent risk of serious harm, the report is assigned a same day response time. These reports may require the involvement of law enforcement. If the report does not allege a child is in imminent risk of serious harm, DCF must respond within 72 hours excluding weekends and holidays. If the report alleges that a child may be in need of services for reasons not related to maltreatment, DCF shall respond within 20 working days.

Q: When may a law enforcement officer remove the child from his or her home?

A: A law enforcement officer is authorized to remove the child from the location where the child is found if the officer reasonably believes that the child is in imminent danger. DCF may not remove the child from a location without a court order. However, DCF can contact law enforcement agencies if the child is in immediate physical danger. Go to www. kscac.org and link to "CACs in Kansas" (Children's Advocacy Center) for a current map of CAC service areas.

Q: What is the DCF response to child abuse and neglect following investigation?

A: Services for prevention and treatment of child abuse may be provided by DCF and other community resources to children and families such as: intensive in-home services, family preservation services, in-home visits, parenting classes, foster care, referrals to mental health centers, drug and alcohol treatment, and Batterer's Intervention Programs. It is always the goal of DCF to maintain children with their families when this can be done safely.

CHAPTER 13

A Guide for Discussion

THE BLUEBONNET FLOWER GROWS in very poor soil. One would never guess this truth but the bright, proud bonnets tell no lies. Not even unkempt soil can keep a Bluebonnet from producing its lovely blossoms.

People can be similar to the Bluebonnet flower. They are born into poor soil and have to live with the challenges presented to them. Children from neglectful or abusive families are Bluebonnet Children.

We are trained in Children and Family Ministry that the parent is the primary faith nurturer. But what happens to a child who does not have a healthy parent to nourish them?

It is at these moments when the local church steps up as a supplemental family. While doing their best to include the parents, the Body of Christ adopts the Triple A Approach. This is Biblically based and is backed by the social sciences. It equips them as they become vessels that shower a Bluebonnet Child with God's grace. This approach calls them to: be aware, to advocate, and to articulate in the child's life. With the Holy Spirit's help, they can become more *aware* of the child's story, *advocate* for her needs, and theologically *articulate* how the healing power of Christ is at work in her life. While this work is heavy, in Christ there is hope.

CHAPTER 1

1. Whose face came to mind as you read this chapter? Who is the Bluebonnet Child in your midst?

2. How would your next interaction with a child be different if you viewed him or her as a, "young disciple of today on her path to becoming tomorrow's spiritual healthy adult?"

3. What "vibes" does a Bluebonnet Child get as he or she enters your church doors?

CHAPTER 2

1. Is there a part of your story that forever altered your perspective in ministry? What fruit has been born from this mentality shift?

2. How could your story offer healing to another? A fellow teammate? A child? A family member? An acquaintance you have yet to meet?

3. What would happen if the Bluebonnet Child in your midst knew you prayed for him or her? How might he/she act if he or she knew you *earnestly* believed he or she was *more* than a conqueror through Christ?

CHAPTER 3

1. How do *prescriptive* (Deuteronomy 6:4–9, Matthew 28:16–20, Philippians 4:13) Biblical texts compare to *descriptive* (1 Kings 11:3, 1 Corinthians 14:34, Colossians 4:1) texts? Can you think of any other examples of either?

2. What evidence exists that God was *still* at work despite the darkness of Tamar's story? Where is the grace? Where is the healing?

3. We know not all manuscripts were canonized into our Holy Scriptures. If any details are shared about a person's life in a Biblical scene, we know we should pay *extra* close attention because these moments are rare. What is the significance of Elizabeth and Zechariah's story (Luke 1) as loving, faithful, and intentional parenting "making the cut?" Why did the author feel the need to describe their faithful dynamics? Is there any relationship to this and the grand arrival in the following chapter (Luke 2)?

CHAPTER 4

1. Who in your life built you up as the "church of today" as a child?

2. Was the number of times children are mentioned in the Bible surprising to you? What can you infer from the presence of children in the early church movement?

3. How can Jesus' view of "family" be compared to how your church views "family"?

CHAPTER 5

1. How would you summarize the ecological systems theory?

2. How do these psychological theories affect you as you move forward in serving Bluebonnet Children?

3. When have you served a Bluebonnet Family that fully trusted in your church's ministry? Share this story. What steps made this a healthy and helpful relationship?

CHAPTER 6

1. What is an alternative way to handle the "baby in the kitchen sink" situation? Can you compose a conversation between you and Leslie?

2. What would have happened if the caretakers had not taken the time to bathe Jeremy, feed him better, and simply voice their concern?

3. Who on your children's ministry team could you see going above and beyond in the same exact way with a child?

CHAPTER 7

1. Are you aware of your gifts (talents) and limitations? How could you better honor both of these?

2. What does your ideal regimen of prayer look like? How do you operate differently when you are fully in tune with the Holy Spirit?

3. Think of a time in your ministry when a lack of awareness toward a person's story (all of the internal and external factors at play) negatively affected the situation. Looking back, offer a solution for a better outcome. Send up a prayer for those involved.

CHAPTER 8

1. What are some of your own conversational tactics when striving to partner with a Bluebonnet Parent? What would happen if you were to adopt the "sidle up" method for your next conversation with a difficult parent?

2. What unique needs would your Safety Policy need to address to best protect the children, volunteers and overall reputation of your church's ministry?

3. What are the pros and cons for a Bluebonnet Child in the two main schools of thought on Children's Church? If you were to design the ideal worship service for Bluebonnet Children, what would it look like?

CHAPTER 9

1. Out of your church family, what percent realize their divine obligation (and privilege) to narrate the sacredness of life to younger disciples? Why do you think this is?

2. Which is more important for a teacher in your programs, to possess sound theology or the ability to "read a room" and empathize with the learners? Why?

3. Can you defend the importance of faith milestones? Which ones does your church offer? Which ones would you like to add?

CHAPTER 10

1. In these three stories of promise, what evidence is there that someone was aware of their poor soil?

2. How would you describe the steps of advocacy in each story?

3. Can you recall who articulated how the Spirit was moving in each story? If one of these Bluebonnet Children was part of your church family, what would you have spoken into their young hearts?

CHAPTER 11

1. How many Bluebonnet Children are present or mentioned in this scene?

2. How does the following quote from Jamie's dad relate to the stories of most Bluebonnet Children, "Jamie, I understand. You hate me because I ran away. How is going in that room any different? Is that what you want? To be like me?"

3. Jamie's mom pours out this beautiful battle cry of parenting. It is truly an explosion of joy and sacrificial love. It is fierce. It is enduring. If you were to create a similar mantra or a piece of visual art to show your utter commitment to the Bluebonnet Child, what would this look like? Jamie is her adopted son; please pause and pray for the children in foster programs. Please share your mantra, artwork, or prayers on social media by tagging it with #bluebonnetchild.

CHAPTER 12

1. Why do so few people "say something" when they "see something?"

2. What does one have to lose by picking up the phone?

3. Is there a Bluebonnet Child who needs you to "Follow *the* call and make a call?"

Bibliography

Berk, Laura E. *Development Through the Lifespan*. 3rd ed. Boston: Pearson, 2004.

Cherry, Kendra. *The Everything Psychology Book*. Avon, AdamsMedia, 2014.

Clinton, Robert and Paul Stanley. *Connecting; The Mentoring Relationships You Need to Succeed in Life*. Carol Streams: NavPress, 1992.

DeVol, Philip E. et al. *Bridges Out of Poverty: Strategies for Professionals and Communities*. Highlands: aha! Process, Inc. 1996.

Folgelson-Teel, Marni. "Baltimore School Deals with Conflict by Sending kids to the Mindful Moments Room Instead of the Principal's' Office." http://www.inhabitots.com

Frazer, Karen, "Charities of Oprah Winfrey". http://charity.lovetoknow.com/Charities_of_Oprah_Winfrey#3c08cmVwjho1ECJk.97

Garland, David E and Diana R Garland. *Flawed Families of the Bible*. Grand Rapids: Brazos, 2007.

Hollands, Iain. "You Me, and the Apocalypse; Home Sweet Home". NBC/Sky 1, New York City. 3 March 2016. Television. http://www.springfieldspringfield.co.uk/view_episode_scripts.php?tv-show=you-me-andtheapocalypse-2015&episode=s01e06

Jensen, Eric. *Teaching with the Brain in Mind*. Vermont. ASCD, 2005.

The Kansas Department of Children and Families. *A Guide to Reporting Child Abuse and Neglect*, Topeka: The State of Kansas Division of Printing, 2016

Lambert, Shawn. "A Christian Perspective on Attention, Awareness, and Mindfulness." *Mind and Soul* (2013) : www.mindandsoul.info.

Notable Biographies: *The Biography of Oprah Winfrey*. http://notablebiographies.com/we-z/winfrey-oprah.html

Ong, Czarina. "Why Dear Younger Me is the Hardest Song They Ever Had to Write. "*http://www.christiantoday.com*.

On-line. http://www.beadisciple.com

On-line. http://www.eaglenestinc.org

On-line. http://safegatherings.com

Pauley, Judith A, et al. *Here's How to Reach Me; Matching Instruction to Personality Types in Your Classroom.* Baltimore: Paul H.Brookes, 2002.

Stonehouse, Catherine. *Joining Children on the Spiritual Journey; Nurturing a Life of Faith.* Grand Rapids: Baker Publishing House, 1998,170.

Toomer, Jessica, "Matt Redman on Fatherhood, faith and Unbroken Faith" *https://www.guideposts.org*

Wax, Ruby. *A Mindfulness Guide for the Frazzled.* London: Penguin, 2016.

Whittaker, Todd. *Dealing with Difficult Parents.* New York City: Routledge, 2016.

———. *What Great Teachers do Differently: 17 Things That Matter Most 2nd ed..* Oxon: Routledge, 2012.

Zuck, Roy. *Precious in His Sight: Childhood and Children in the Bible.* Grand Rapids: Baker Academic, 1996.